ALL
THE
WRONG
MOVES

ALL
THE
WRONG
MOVES

A Memoir About Chess, Love, and Ruining Everything

SASHA CHAPIN

Doubleday
New York

Copyright © 2019 by Alexander Chapin

All rights reserved. Published in the United States by
Doubleday, a division of Penguin Random House LLC,
New York. Simultaneously published in Canada by McClelland &
Stewart, an imprint of Random House of Canada, a division of
Penguin Random House Canada Limited, Toronto.

www.doubleday.com

DOUBLEDAY and the portrayal of an anchor with a dolphin
are registered trademarks of Penguin Random House LLC.

Jacket art references a photograph by Nilotic / Shutterstock
Jacket art and design by Emily Mahon

Title page art © Sangu_rabi / Shutterstock
Chapter opener art © valterZ / Shutterstock

Library of Congress Cataloging-in-Publication Data
Names: Chapin, Sasha, author.
Title: All the wrong moves : a memoir about chess,
love, and ruining everything / Sasha Chapin.
Description: First edition. | New York : Doubleday, [2019]
Identifiers: LCCN 2019000510 (print) |
LCCN 2019007679 (ebook) | ISBN 9780385545181 (ebook) |
ISBN 9780385545174 (hardcover)
Subjects: LCSH: Chapin, Sasha. | Chess players—Canada—
Biography. | Chapin, Sasha—Travel. | Chess—Tournaments.
Classification: LCC GV1439.C42 (ebook) |
LCC GV1439.C42 A3 2019 (print) | DDC 794.1092—dc23
LC record available at https://lccn.loc.gov/2019000510

MANUFACTURED IN THE UNITED STATES OF AMERICA

1 3 5 7 9 10 8 6 4 2

First Edition

CONTENTS

ALL
THE
WRONG
MOVES

THE 600 MILLION

Perhaps the surest sign that you're in love is that you can't stop talking. You find yourself announcing the name of your beloved at the slightest provocation. Given any opportunity, you engage in a vain attempt to explain your infatuation. Everything else seems unworthy of a single moment's attention or discussion. No matter how shy or stoic you are, real affection demands expression.

And this is no less true when the object of your affection is the game of chess. In other words, when you're me.

But this poses a bit of a problem. It's tricky to explain the appeal of chess to someone who doesn't play. Unlike the beauty of other sports, the majesty of chess is somewhat opaque to the uninitiated. Basketball, I'm sure, has infinitesimal subtleties I can't fully appreciate, but when I'm watching a game, I can still sense that LeBron is doing something really cool. The sheer physicality is imposing—the taut calves, the curves carved in the air by the ball meeting the basket. Not so with chess. All you do is look at two nerds staring at a collection of tiny figurines.

And yet, my love of chess demands that I continue, that I somehow communicate why chess captivates me in ways that nothing else ever could. Why I've neglected food, sex, and friendship, on many an occasion, for its charms. Why nothing—not love, not amphetamines, not physical danger—makes my heart beat harder than the process of cornering an opponent's king.

If you think this is crazy, I agree. But it deserves mentioning that I'm not the only crazy one. Albert Einstein and Humphrey Bogart were similarly affected by the thirty-two pieces on the sixty-four squares. And, some centuries before that, Caliph Muhammad al-Amin, ruler of the Abbasid empire, insisted on continuing a promising endgame as marauders penetrated his throne room, decapitating him shortly after he delivered checkmate.

I didn't get decapitated, so my affair with chess really wasn't so bad. All I got was the total consumption of my soul.

Like so many affairs, it began with an accidental flirtation that became an all-devouring union—two years during which I did little else but pursue chess mastery. Despite my obvious lack of talent, I leapt across continents to play in far-flung competitions, studied with an eccentric grandmaster, spent almost all of my money, neglected my loved ones, and accumulated a few infections. And I did it all for a brief shot at glory—a chance to take down some real players at a tournament in Los Angeles, where my place in humanity was determined, as far as I'm concerned.

Maybe if you come back with me, through those nights of chasing imaginary kings with imaginary queens, along my winding road to the San Fernando Valley, you'll understand my love of chess. Maybe you'll even understand why, according to recent estimates, one in twelve people in the world plays chess in some capacity. Maybe you'd like to know what's been captivating well over 600 million souls while you were doing whatever you do.

Frankly, I didn't feel like I was doing much until chess came along. Sure, there were momentary rages, dwindling loves, and, occasionally, a charming vista. But it was all part of an unformed sequence of anecdotes, through which I was stumbling sideways, grasping at whatever I could, whether it was some form of self-destruction or a nice afternoon walk. By contrast, when chess appeared, it felt like a possession—like a spirit had slipped a long finger up through my spine, making me a marionette, pausing only briefly to ask, "You weren't doing anything with *this,* were you?"

1

KATHMANDU

Anyway, like most people, I became obsessed with chess after I ran away to Asia with a stripper I'd just met.

Courtney made an impression. Before I saw her face, at the poetry reading where we encountered each other, I heard the precise, cutting melody of her voice sailing above the room's otherwise meek murmurs. And as soon as I saw her, it became clear, from both the way she looked and the way that everyone else looked at her, that she was the unelected supervisor of that evening. She had one of those sharp smiles that you could easily imagine encircling the necks of her enemies. She was slim and pale, with severe good looks. Everything she wore was obviously expensive: shiny black boots, shiny black pants, and an extravagantly fluffy white sweater that shed hairs everywhere. The room around her slowly became dandered.

Even before we spoke, her presence added a little bit

of much-needed electricity to the otherwise un-fascinating evening. The poetry reading was boring. And I went there knowing I would be bored, because I didn't care about experimental poetry. But I figured that I should go for vague professional reasons. I had recently started a career as a freelance writer, having published a couple of sensitive essays that had earned modest local acclaim. And in my mind this meant, somehow, that attending tedious literary events was now my sacred responsibility.

She and I met when I started flirting with a friend of hers, whose social pleasantness I mistakenly took for some sort of invitation. Courtney saved me from embarrassment by swooping in and derailing the conversation with an avalanche of pointed queries and cleverly backhanded compliments. At first, I had no idea whether she liked me or could even tolerate my presence. She seemed entirely self-contained, like there wasn't anything I could possibly add to her life, which may have been true. I asked her what she thought of the poetry, expecting a mushy statement of reverence of the sort I'd received from everyone else I'd asked that question.

"It was mostly shitty," she said.

After a few minutes, I got a little better at keeping up with the staccato conversational rhythm that was her specialty, but I still felt nervous. Until, that is, she started massaging my knee under the table, apropos of nothing, after we had consumed a helpful amount of alcohol.

Following our first intimate moments, a few days later, I told her that it kind of sucked that we hadn't encountered each other earlier, because I was moving overseas in two weeks. When she asked me why, I told her the same silly thing I told everybody: I was going away to Thailand so I could write in solitude. At this early stage in my career, I said, I should devote myself to my craft, rather than deal with the constant distractions of my busy life in Toronto. Whether or not I believed this myself I'm not sure, but it was obviously untrue. Writing was going well. I was producing at a reasonable rate, and I was getting paid pretty generously.

Moreover, since I had never been alone in an unknown country, I had no reason to suspect that it would improve me in any way. Really, the decision was based on fear. I'm kind of an insecure person, and whenever I'm stationary in life for more than a few moments—whenever I'm settled in any lifestyle at all—I start becoming suspicious of the validity of my very being. In this case, I couldn't stomach the fact of remaining in Toronto, getting paid to put my feelings on the Internet while working at a fancy pasta restaurant. There had to be something more out there, something more noble or treacherous. And while I did have some good friends in the city, I wasn't entirely sure why they liked me anymore. Perhaps the decisive factor, finally, was that I had some money saved up, which traditionally means that I'm about to do something stupid.

"I wonder if I'm so attracted to you just because you're leaving," Courtney said, over dinner a week later.

"I'm like a rare postage stamp," I said.

"I don't know why I just told you that."

"That you're attracted to me just because I'm unavailable?"

"Yeah."

"Well, at least you're attracted to me."

Later, a few drinks further along, she suggested that we should do drugs together so she could puzzle out exactly what she felt about me—specifically *Psilocybe cubensis,* aka magic mushrooms.

"Like, right now?" I said.

"Yeah, sure."

I agreed. We walked back to my apartment. After choking down a strong dose of twisty green-gray magic mushrooms, we sat in my living room, awaiting the first bloom of a long high. Following the brief anxiety that you feel when you're awaiting intoxication, the walls got wiggly. Somehow, we started believing that the couch was a condom. Water, we decided, was actually rock juice. Great, nonsensical insight flew off the walls, hitting us hard in the head. Out in the cool night air, she told me all about how her lamb's brambles were scrambled. The wind blew up the dust from a lawn we found.

"This is why I didn't go to college," she said.

"Because it was too windy?" I said.

"Yeah."

We took a cab home and went to bed at 6 a.m., agreeing that it was fun being alive, considering how anyone could bomb you, at any time, for any reason or no reason at all. When we woke up at noon, she said she was thinking of asking me whether she could come with me.

"You should," I said.

"Why?" she said.

"Because I'd say yes."

"Can I come with you?"

"Yeah, sure."

Having figured that out, we got some greasy breakfast at the corner diner.

Doing shrooms with somebody instantly acquaints you with about half of who they are. When someone is on shrooms, they're taken over by unalloyed emotionality— by the things they suppress so that they can participate in civilization. And this is a great bonding experience, but you do run a certain risk you can trick yourself into thinking you've seen their essential soul, when, really, the whimsy they keep inside isn't any more real than the more polished elements on the surface. Essentially, I knew Courtney's inside more than I knew her outside. To each of us, the other was an intimately familiar stranger.

Courtney's drug-induced crush on me wasn't the only reason a sudden departure was appealing. She hated the club she worked at. Also, her ex-boyfriend had returned to

Toronto after living away for a while, and he was apparently monitoring us, as evidenced by the fact that soon after we started hanging out, he texted her an inquiry about whether "the guy in the green coat" was any good in bed, in reference to my long forest-green duffel. It all looked like a big blinking exit sign. After breakfast, she booked a ticket on my flight.

"Is this crazy?" she said.

"Yeah, definitely," I said.

"What if we break up?"

"I think maybe there's about a fifty-fifty chance that we'll break up almost immediately."

She found those terms acceptable. Seventy-two hours later, we were in Shanghai, fleeing an Australian man the size of a tractor, who took Courtney's lack of fondness very personally. As we rounded a corner, Courtney was attacked by a street hustler's pet monkey.

That was our layover in China. After we escaped, we rented a little apartment in Chiang Mai, a smallish city in the north of Thailand. If you're a sufficiently wealthy foreigner living in Chiang Mai, you'll find yourself in a perfect place, and maybe get a little bored, and start wondering whether perfection is everything you want in life. There's a lot to like and not much to do. It's a touristy student town with a bunch of temples.

That was just fine with me. A small city where I could coast in unconcern was exactly what I needed. Every day, I went to the library, pretended I was writing for four hours, wrote for two hours, and then met up with Courtney, who loved Chiang Mai, too, at first. She laughed and screamed and sighed at all the bright novelty around her. And her presence made me a more exciting person, because I wanted to demonstrate my daring. If I were alone, I might have quietly pursued my low-energy occupation. Instead, I assiduously sought out and strip-mined the few local sources of adventure. I drove us around on a tiny, fast motorbike, through congested traffic, out of the city on winding and unmarked roads, and then up and down forested mountains. We ate grilled ribs from market stalls on the edge of town, bathed in streams, and got lost whenever we could.

But Courtney grew discontented. She'd escaped from the catastrophes she'd been dealing with, but now she was actually in another place—in this case, a half-bland paradise where she could spend long periods of time staring at her fingernails and ignoring the distant scrape of oblivion. During the daytime, she loved the spicy food and the fragrant swelter, but the empty evenings were boring at best. It was a lifestyle with no obvious purpose or an obvious way to pass the time. Chiang Mai had about three weeks' worth of fun in it, and we'd been there for about three weeks. Our conversations grew thin, until we spent a lot of our alone time silently drinking Chang beer. Chang instills a distinctive hangover and tastes like discarded friendships. I became sullen and Courtney became moody and erratic.

Since we were going crazy, I suggested we take a trip to Bangkok, Thailand's capital, which is literally the hottest city on the planet. The heat feels like reality is exaggerating. It's like, come on, really? Are you serious? As soon as you step off the plane, the molten air viciously massages your entire body. During the evenings, a hot wind sweeps away the daytime. It's a terrible, loud, hectic city that we both adored immediately. After Chiang Mai's sensory deprivation, we welcomed all the sensory abrasion Bangkok imposed—even the smell, which I might describe as the scent of a cream puff served on garbage. Among the odors, we sat on a rooftop, drinking even more Chang, watching the sun sail down through the roseate smog. "We should live here," Courtney said, as the skyline declared its supremacy over the arriving night. I agreed.

The next day, we walked through a pleasant neighborhood called Ari, a hive of royalists, young professionals, and the people who feed them chicken and cockles. The street was a lovely mess of vendors selling soup, tailoring, and flowers. Friends yelled at each other merrily, and pigeons sunbathed on the balustrades of low-rise apartments. It seemed like a good place to find a residence. But since I didn't know anybody in Bangkok, I had no idea how you would go about navigating that process. Accordingly, I stopped two young women at random and inquired about the local real-estate situation. We all went for coffee, and one of them, an extroverted NGO worker named Elena, was looking for a roommate to replace the other, a witty reporter named Sally, who was moving out of their apartment. I told them that Courtney and I might be that roommate, so Elena took us back to a draughty, rambling floor of an old gray tenement that possessed an irresistible and shambolic charm. We put down rent.

But a problem presented itself: Courtney was almost bankrupt. She announced that she'd fly home and work two weeks of double shifts at the club, which would get her enough cash to keep us full of Chang for a long time. As soon as she presented this plan, I suspected that she wouldn't come back. The limitations of our relationship had become clear—it seemed like a good idea while we were on drugs, but she didn't really know what she was doing in Thailand, and neither did I. We'd developed a kind of love for each other, but it wasn't quite enough that it all made sense.

She left just before Christmas, so I was alone on New Year's Eve in our Chiang Mai apartment, after flying back to collect my belongings. Every New Year's Eve in Chiang Mai they fill the sky with thousands of floating lanterns. This is some beautiful religious tradition that probably dates back millions of years. You set the sky on fire so you can watch it grow back as spring comes. Lying on my small, firm, bare bed, I observed the flocks of tiny flames filling the window.

On New Year's Day, when I was flying to Bangkok, everything felt unreal. I was moving to a city about which I knew nearly nothing, on a continent in which I knew two people, pursuing a somewhat tenuous career as a writer, at the end of a somewhat illusory romantic relationship. The only thing that was completely clear was that the flight attendants employed by Thai Airways were impeccably trained, although the food they served was a little too gelatinous for comfort. What was I going to be here? I had suspicions, but really, I had no idea.

When my plane touched down, I was completely alone—Elena was on a jaunt in Myanmar. I got off the rail link from the airport and arrived at an empty home. Truly being without company for the first time was exhilarating, for about four beautiful days where I walked alone in the sprawling city. I was adrift in crowds for a moment or two, then unnerved by the emptiness of an alleyway, then followed by little packs of amiable, dirty street dogs. Sitting down at a noodle stand I found in a distant parking lot amid crumbling high-rises, south of the city's shimmering Chinatown, I felt like the world couldn't possibly contain all the convolutions inside me.

But my baseless reverie crumbled. Without anyone I could sort the diverse new sensations with, or find shelter from the buttery light with, it all seemed a little wasted. Shortly, I wanted to fall off the earth. Bathed in soot, I bought pomelos in solitude, watching happy Thai couples chit-chat.

Like many white people before me, I was becoming

bored in Asia. And I wasn't writing much of anything. What I found out, almost immediately, was that it's hard for me to write if I don't have people around whom I might delight or dismay. I live for approval. I'm just a dancing bear, fundamentally. But being in Bangkok was all about being on a Skytrain shoulder to shoulder with hundreds of people who couldn't read my stupid little thoughts even if they wanted to. There was a big empty in my head. Days crawled, somehow not only large with boring white minutes, but also small as they disappeared without a trace. Barely understanding Thai, I floated in a sea of incomprehensible murmurs; occasionally I overheard one of the maybe one hundred words in my vocabulary. "Oh," I would think, "someone is discussing pork." In January I was writing six pieces at once, but in February I was barely writing one. My credit card balance crept up; I observed it with no particular emotion. And as I predicted, there was no sign of Courtney.

That's when my troubles really started. Or not then exactly, but right after, when Elena got back from a trip to Nepal. That's when life as I now know it began. Not that I knew that at the time. The future never announces itself. Your destiny is quietly prepared offstage, until the hour when it emerges, saying something like, "Knock knock, motherfucker." Elena arrived in the apartment bearing a contagious excitation about the most recent leg of her travels.

"Nepal is so interesting," she said.

"What's going on there?" I said.

"There's a blockade, gasoline isn't making it over the Indian border, nobody can do anything, and, like, everything is paralyzed."

"That sounds good."

"The weather is really good right now, too."

"Should I write a story about it?"

"Totally."

So I did—a story about the incredibly complicated domestic tensions there, which I barely understood, even after extensive research. Essentially all I knew was that reporters should talk to people, so from the moment I landed in Kathmandu, I began a conversation with everyone who engaged me in more than a moment of eye contact. During this ungainly process, after ambling down an arbitrary lane, I found myself in a rubble-strewn square presided over by a group of chess hustlers—strong players who make their salary on small-wager games with suckers like me. Around the board stood a small, silent crowd, which I immediately joined, attempting to be inconspicuous. Despite my efforts, though, everyone noticed the presence of a non-Nepali, so the crowd's focus shifted towards me. After the conclusion of the game I'd interrupted, they all wondered aloud whether I might join in. I said, "Um, golly, uh, sure, okay, why not?" then sat down on the dusty stone across from my opponent, whose name was Tenjing.

He opened the game in the most common fashion, by

playing e4.* This was the only opening move Bobby Fischer enjoyed playing: he called it "best by test." In response, I played the move e6—the first move of the French Defense.

The French Defense was an old friend of mine that I hadn't seen since I was a teenager. I hardly recognized it when I saw it on the board, although we had once been intimately familiar. It was my weapon of choice when I played on my hippie alternative school's chess team, the Pawnishers.

---

* This is how chess moves are abbreviated: "[piece] [destination square]." The squares are denoted by a number and a letter, which refer, respectively, to their vertical and horizontal—the board stretches between a1, at the lower left, and h8, at the upper right. When a capture happens, the word *takes* is inserted—e.g., "bishop takes h3." If it's a pawn move, only the destination square is included: "e4," for example. Also, this is the last footnote in this book, I promise.

THE PAWNISHERS

To get at what chess meant to me as an adolescent, unfortunately I have to tell you a little bit about my childhood. Specifically, there's one piece of information I should convey, which is the fact that nobody liked me, and that they were probably right not to like me. I was an annoying and abrasive person, constantly ranting and raving and demanding attention from others, and whining and crying when I couldn't get it. Prepubescent me was notable for two things: an expansive vocabulary and the way I irritated people by spraying my surroundings with it.

As much as it might have seemed so, I didn't want to be disliked. What I wanted was to communicate my constant excitement about all the slivers of reality I could touch and gather with my overactive mind. Nearly everything thrilled me. Sometimes I would become so possessed by my private thicket of thoughts and associations that I'd start sprinting down the street, chased by some fulminating notion, and would often collide with a mailbox or a stranger. Like instantly blooming clutches of bougainvillea, refractions of the world sprang all over my insides, and I wanted to get them out. But the only result of this instinct was my social unacceptability.

At a very young age, this meant I didn't have much fun on the playground. Nobody wanted to play with me, so I dug through soil on the edge of the schoolyard and watched insects squirm through my fingers. A few years after that, my isolation was replaced by vicious, constant bullying, administered by beautiful young men who were finding their manhood through the enforcement of pubescent tribal boundaries, outside of which I always fell. Each day at school was a long torture, during which every one of my outward behaviors—the way I chewed, talked, or walked—was cruelly mimicked by the most popular children. At one point, I happened to inhale as a boy named Troy was passing in front of my chair. He accused me of trying to smell his butt, and for the rest of that year, I was "the butt-sniffer," and I was greeted by exaggerated sniffing noises every time I entered a room.

This gave me a pervasive shame: a feeling that the project of my very being had been given failing marks by some invisible and final council. And this shame never really disappeared completely, and in fact only abated slightly, even as my social standing improved.

Which it did, considerably: as my teenage years continued, I pieced together something of a halfway-acceptable personality, by imitating public radio hosts and the more charismatic neurotics in Woody Allen movies. After doing well on some standardized tests, I was placed in a class for the academically gifted, which was slightly less dominated by jocks. Thereafter, I slipped further towards the margins, to an alternative school called Inglenook, which was filled with hippies and eccentrics and stoners, among whom I wasn't considered totally malformed. In fact, by the time I was sixteen or so, some of the boys thought I was interesting, if trying, and some of the girls thought I was cute.

But the shame marred all of this completely. During any social situation, I was constantly suppressing the silent terror that, at any moment, the ruse of my charm would disappear, and that the friendliness or toleration displayed by my peers would become menace. When a pretty young woman deigned to take my pants off, I managed to enjoy what followed, but would often afterwards be seized with the certainty that she'd subsequently realize that I was completely disgusting and that our sexual encounter was a mistake.

From the outside, it would seem like I was having fun. My nerdy nature had been corrupted by an aspiration towards delinquency. An evening spent pursuing my preferences might end with public indecency committed with a near-stranger atop an unmoored train car. Frequently, I trespassed for recreation—I loved traipsing around abandoned buildings, or swimming in public pools after hours, or sneaking around fancy hotels. And I was getting cozy with a few drugs. But it was all an attempt at filling an extremely durable void. Nights spent chasing novelty and the opposite sex were what I had instead of self-esteem or a purpose.

That's when the Pawnishers, the Inglenook chess team, came in.

The Pawnishers were brought together by Liam, a boy who could bend the world to his will. Everywhere he went, a situation began. This is perhaps best exemplified by the fact that he somehow had an Internet fan base who held a real life convention in his honor. They, a dozen or so people, flew him out to Virginia, just so they could get him drunk and make out with him in shallow, cold water. He was influential like that. So, when he informed the bookish contingent of the school that they were in his chess club, we basically all agreed to this interpretation of our lives.

I think, at first, I did it just because I wanted to belong to some kind of cadre. Having a ready-made, highly ostentatious identity was socially useful, especially in a school composed of total freaks. Our school, as previously mentioned, was an asylum. The most popular girls, a trio of charming blondes with outrageously colorful outfits, would announce nonchalantly that they were on LSD during lunch break—excuse me, one would say, I can't really pay attention to what you're saying, because the walls are melting. Our most popular boy, meanwhile, took breaks from meditating in the courtyard to inform everyone who'd listen about the benefits of drinking their own urine. Briefly, I sat next to a young schizoid genius who would rattle off long monologues about Nikola Tesla before announcing his intention to masturbate all over the far wall. He was expelled because of something horrific we were never told about. I saw him last on the steps of a downtown halfway house.

In this druggy, chaotic context, where people were constantly starting bands with names like "Skullfucker," being a chess player was cool and conspicuous. It was counter-counter-culture. However, after the first few weeks of practices, being a Pawnisher started being way more than a self-imposed quirk, because chess was starting to take over my mind.

It had a profound effect on me. I lost interest in all of my other typical activities. The brief thrills of breaking the law or almost breaking a condom felt like shallow flutters compared to the sustained joy of playing over one of Bobby Fischer's masterpieces. Skipping school lost its appeal. Every day, I eagerly awaited the chance to show the other Pawnishers what I'd learned about the game from Wikipedia or an online skirmish.

And when I played chess, I felt, like, different. On the chessboard, the shame that plagued me was temporarily dispelled. It had something to do with how the game involved both self-expression and self-effacement. When I was playing, I was both myself and not myself. My style was driven by my personality, surely—simply for the sake of being strange,

I was drawn to esoteric, weird strategies, preferring to be a tricky counterpuncher rather than a straightforwardly assertive attacking player. But despite that, the game sort of had nothing to do with me. None of my superficial attributes, which I so hated, translated onto the board. When I was checkmating someone, I shrank in importance compared to the pieces before me. It was as if I had temporarily lost my clumsily foaming mouth, and my nervously searching eyes, and my long greasy hair, and the perfectly normal body I had, which struck me as perfectly repulsive.

But in this ecstatic flight from myself, where was I going, exactly?

Psychologist and author Steven Pinker says something about music that I really like. He calls it "auditory cheesecake." Just like cheesecake is so satisfying because it's more sugary than the foods the taste buds were evolved to experience, music overwhelms eardrums that were designed merely to track the movements of predators and the grunts of our loved ones.

It seems like there's something similar going on with chess. Chess pours pure sugar down cognitive pathways that were originally forged for the sake of simple survival. Our sense of pattern recognition, crucial for making our way under the stars, is tickled when we see lethal potential lurking in an innocuous-looking pawn structure. Our sense of geometry, crucial for anticipating the flight path of a potentially delicious bird, is pushed to its limit when we calculate a complex tactic. And perhaps most importantly, our sense of social status, evolved for the wearying task of navigating the pecking order, finds satisfaction not only in the competition itself but in the hierarchy of the pieces—in the thrill we feel when our queen savages its inferiors on our opponent's team.

Also, life has so much waiting in it, know what I mean? You're always waiting for somebody to call, or waiting to fall asleep, or waiting to see whether any of your little plans will ever work out. In chess, though, from the very first move, the players present each other with bold impositions and insane demands, making choices of instant consequence. Fully half the board is occupied by the pieces at the start of the game—there's really no empty space to speak of. Inexorably, the players immediately create a convoluted havoc.

I wasn't great at that havoc, to be honest. I lost almost every competitive game I played. Most of us lost almost every competitive game we played. We were up against kids who'd been playing since they were seven—terribly serious children in unwrinkled school uniforms who said markedly little. They beat us perhaps 80 percent of the time. We just weren't trained the way they were. They were the glossy, efficient nerds, and we were the other kind—scrappy, messy, and precocious in our attainment of bad habits.

We didn't particularly care. Winning was good if it was available, but since it wasn't, we took pleasure in simply being obnoxious. Our signature attire was black-and-white chess-themed war paint with black-and-white vintage clothing, but we sometimes varied our attire, such as during our match against Upper Canada College, the city's snottiest private school for boys. To that game we wore fairly convincing drag. When we arrived, just as class was letting out, we stood on a snowdrift in front of the main entrance, all in colorful gowns, staring salaciously at the student body as it entered its parents' cars. Later, our team's best player, Isaac, absentmindedly fondled his huge prosthetic tits after sliding his bishop through his opponent's defenses. His psychological warfare was remarkably effective—he scored a gigantic upset on his opponent, who was otherwise undefeated that season.

Isaac was a stoner who was a fierce, efficient player when he wasn't stoned, which was almost never. On weed, he was still the best we had. Being beaten by Isaac was especially infuriating because he seemed like he didn't really care about winning. The only sign he gave of preferring a specific outcome was occasional, low-key trash talk delivered with a terrible Russian accent. "Take the pawn, comrade," he would say, in situations where you really shouldn't take the pawn. He had a little catchphrase that became the whole team's mantra: "It's mostly fine." He said it when his game was going terribly, when his opponent was approaching absolute triumph: "It's mostly fine." To this day, in my most hapless moments, when I'm helplessly watching one of my trivial enterprises fall apart, I think, "It's mostly fine."

Though my team's conduct at the board was sometimes dubious, my love of the game became increasingly serious. Along with being emotionally comforting, chess let me display what I felt was my obviously superior mind. Back then, although I still didn't like myself, I was sure I had one redeeming feature: being smarter than everyone else on earth. While I had spent my life up until that point displaying my intellect indirectly—by carrying around big stacks of books or using Latin abbreviations on Microsoft Messenger, that kind of kabuki approach was a little indirect. However, in chess, I could effectively smash my brain directly against someone else's and enjoy the resulting explosions.

...

Learning serious chess is, at first, an exhilarating, emboldening experience. Early on, the novice rapidly conquers conceptual plateaus, easily doubling their skill level, then redoubling it. You start beating players who were equal competition just recently—maybe your cousin, or your podiatrist. They become fearful of your wrath.

After you get a sense of how the pieces move, you then proceed towards an overall understanding of the game's architecture. Generally, each game possesses three stages—however, like life, which is made up of the tripartite sections of kid, old person, then really old person, the categories are porous and their progression may be prematurely halted by stupidity.

The opening is where you maneuver your forces such that you might effectively endanger your opponent—think of the way war used to be fought, with smelly men in big heavy coats arranging themselves before a corresponding row of similarly miserable people, preparing for attack. You place your pieces so they can move effectively—while bishops on their starting square do nearly nothing, when properly led, they slice easily across the whole board. Here, you get an edge by studying "opening theory," which is just a fancy way of saying that you learn how people have begun chess games before, and then move the same way. It's a little bit like learning common chord progressions before you write a song.

Many of the openings have intriguing names—there's the Sicilian Dragon, a century-old standby, or maybe the quirky Réti Opening, if you feel like being a little eccentric. You might learn the Flick-Knife Attack if your opponent has opted for the risky Benoni Defense. If you're crazy, you might attempt the Halloween Gambit, where you give up your pieces so you can play in a scary-looking but frivolous fashion. You get deeply involved in the lines of play you might enjoy, so that eventually you might say, as I did, "I've been studying some lines in the accepted Poisoned Pawn Variation of the Winawer French Defense."

Unless you perpetrate a truly grand fuck-up in the opening stages—which is easily possible—you then enjoy the middle-game. During this phase, there are many active pieces on the board, which dance around each other, presenting threats and counter-threats, or perhaps simply murdering each other off the board in pairs. The grand dramas of the game usually take place here, and the personalities of the players become manifest. Aggressive players search for a swift ending, imposing threats both serious and empty, dancing with demoniac energy across spaces they rip open by force and putting their pieces in harm's way with glee. More strategic players, so-called "positional" players, cramp their opponents, seizing little packets of space, asking a series of uncomfortable questions to which the only answers are more or less effective forms of wriggling.

If none of this leads to checkmate, the endgame is reached—the slow grappling of the few pieces still standing. Mostly, the endgame revolves around carefully escorting pawns up the board, since the pawn, upon attaining the square opposite its starting position, becomes a queen, the most powerful piece, an event that usually provokes the sullen handshake that traditionally caps off a game. Endgames are the province of the most scrupulous players—they're often superficially boring, but those who understand their subtleties can swindle those who don't. They're stones that, when squeezed hard enough, often actually do produce blood.

This was the saga playing out every afternoon between members of the Pawnishers—an after-school pack of sweaty teenage boys, giggling about their triumphs, ignoring the warm weather outside. And although my addiction didn't then reach the paralyzing extremity that it eventually would, it did interfere with my non-chess affairs. For example, I was ejected from class by my history teacher for playing chess with myself during a lecture about the emergence of AIDS. She admonished me that I was "wasting my fucking life." And she was correct. That year was a defining moment. The grades I earned would permit or deny access to the universities I applied to. But all of that seemed vague next to a nice checkmating attack. It wasn't so much that I didn't care about the future, but more that I cared about chess much more. And I was in paradise. The camaraderie among the Pawnishers was my daily comfort, and the intricacies of the game were my religion.

Even more importantly, I was finally better than my big brother at something. This had never happened before. When I was little, Sam was simply a better person in every way. He was taller, and he was cuter. During our very young years, he was one of my primary bullies, and continued my social torture after I got home from school. During our later teenage years, he became less vicious (he's now perhaps my closest friend), but he was still obviously my superior: the smartest one in a smart family, a fact that I denied vociferously because I knew it was true. But chess is an acquired skill—a reasonably smart person who'd studied the game, like me, could beat a genius who hadn't done any of the homework, like him. Our rivalry began one night at home, when he interrupted me while I was studying a chess book, playing out positions on a little board in front of the TV. He told me that chess was a silly game. I said, "All right, beat me, then."

Five games later, he was enraged and perplexed. During every game, he made utterly transparent threats, which I easily parried, before checkmating him in ways he hadn't seen coming. He was useless, and shocked by his own uselessness. I had never, ever outshone him in such a casual fashion, or in any fashion at all. My satisfaction was so great that I often let the games go on much longer than they could have. I would get a winning position, then let him wallow in his misery for a dozen moves or so. Then I'd jump my pieces in and destroy him.

Sadly, this state of affairs didn't persist for long. My brother's brain is one of those beautiful logical brains that methodically devours all of what it's exposed to—you can almost feel it whirring when my brother speaks. Meanwhile, I have a lazy, wandering mind. I fritter away hours on long trains of thought, then leave the stove on, nearly burning down my building and killing everyone. Accordingly, Sam brought a meticulousness to the study of chess that I couldn't muster. After he embraced chess for a week, we were almost equals—I could generally beat him, but not easily. A week later, every game was a struggle, where even achieving a survivable position required absolute vigilance. Soon, my brother could effortlessly victimize me with his intellect. Our games were so one-sided that they were boring from a chess perspective. It was fun for him only because he liked watching me suffer.

It became hard to take chess, or myself, seriously at all. I went to school and waited all day to play with the Pawnishers, and then played in a state of melancholy, knowing how limited my skills were. That dreary state persisted until early evening, when I'd go home and my grinning brother would confront me, asking me whether I'd like to play for a little while. Confronted by these circumstances, I gave up chess. Unhappily, I returned to occupying myself with sluttiness and getting high, and feeling that I was essentially deficient.

Although I took a few brief stabs at chess when I was bored, that was basically the end of my career. Chess, apparently, was just one of those things I liked when I was a kid, like cartoons, or Sartre, or weed, things I discarded when I went to university and started attempting adulthood. By the time I met Courtney, it was even further behind me, because I had generally figured out how to like what cool people liked. They liked cocktails, and complaining about modernity, and taking flattering but not too flattering pictures of each other. They certainly didn't like chess, so by the time I left for Thailand, it no longer had anything to do with who I was.

Until I ended up in Kathmandu, with the French Defense before me on the board, by no contrivance I was aware of.

It was a cool, sunny afternoon. The city's ornate architecture was punctuated by piles of rubble generated by the two recent earthquakes. The crowd around the board was enclosed on all sides by the rush of pedestrian traffic. Tenjing smiled at me as we rattled off a few canonical opening moves we'd both seen many times before. He was an assertive player. I was remembering how the pieces moved. But within a few minutes, that old chess feeling was returning— the dizzy pleasure of the potential maneuvers multiplying before you, transforming an idle board of sixty-four black-and-white squares into a tumultuous arena of mental conflict.

Then, he beat me in twenty moves. (Twenty moves is a very short game, forty is a medium one, a hundred is cause for weeping.) Another game rapidly went the same way. The spectators became very pleasant, smiling as they observed me forking over my little wrinkled bills, patting me on the back encouragingly as Tenjing took all my pieces.

Badly played chess is kind of like badly played life. Real problems are dealt with poorly or not at all, while much effort is expended on avoiding imaginary danger. Rather than dealing with the reality of the situation, you act as if you were playing the game you wish you were. Then you collide with the boundaries between the actual and the hypothetical.

At first, that's how I was performing. And, weirdly, I found myself caring about this. I was emotionally involved. My teenage self, the one to whom this game was life, was surprisingly close to the surface. That self felt quite foolish, especially when Tenjing began chatting with the crowd, evidently needing little concentration to wipe me off the board. This was not the dramatically correct version of this scene, in which the mysterious foreigner stuns the people of Kathmandu with his preternatural skill. But about four games in, some long-resting regions in my brain lit up. Somehow I recalled some of my favorite ways of playing the Poisoned Pawn Variation of the Winawer French Defense.

You might say that it's a murder-suicide kind of chess opening. The player with the black pieces starts by generously giving a few delicious pawns to his opponent's hungry queen. This is a strange thing to do, because an extra pawn often decides the game if neither king gets checkmated in the initial stages. However, pawns can also get in the way of an attack—they keep your position secure, but they lock your pieces in as well. They're your trusty, dumb infantry, who gleefully stagger forward until they hit an obstacle and sit on it immovably. By giving some away, you erase the architecture of the board, allowing your forces to gallop all over. Rather than creating conditions under which the game might well be a draw, you pull out a knife and declare that somebody's going to die.

A procession of new emotions took over my opponent's

face. The easy grace of a winner became the intrigue of a slight challenge, which then became the sangfroid of true competition. Our pieces weaved around the board as we carefully anticipated each other's threats. The noise in the street—the chuckle of a motorbike motor, the skittering of rickshaw wheels off hard stone, the trilingual mercantile patter—became as nothing. But, finally, Tenjing beat me very suddenly with a subtle tactic I had not foreseen. After a few moves that seemed nonsensical, my queen was trapped on the edge of the board, where it was easily rounded up.

Without a word, I rose and slunk away, crossing through a bustling market to Ratna Park, a frantic bus depot from which I took a terrifyingly fast trip to an objectively more important event. I had a meeting with a Nepali intellectual with a voice as soft as cool milk, who spoke with quavering eloquence, summarizing centuries of history with carefully turned sentences. With the assured evenness of someone accustomed to sorrow, he told me about the struggle of his marginalized ethnic group, which had been exploited by the ruling class of the country. He was impressive, and important, and I felt that I had become slightly more impressive and important for being in his presence, in a faraway land, mining information that could lessen humankind's suffering if I paraphrased it well enough.

And I was surprised to find that I essentially didn't give a fuck about impressiveness, or importance, or any of it at all. As I sat there on his patio, drinking tea brought to us by his wife, I realized that all I really wanted to do was go back to the square and eloquently marginalize Tenjing's pieces. After I dutifully completed the interview, carefully concealing my lack of interest, I went back to my hotel room and lay awake, smoking in bed, thinking about the game's final position. Occasionally, I took my rumination out onto the veranda, from which I saw the total dark of the street broken by the dangling of flashlights. There I was, above the soil of a country torn apart by seismic activity, below the skyward plunge of perfect mountains, on the night before setting out for the southern wetlands, where police were having a fun time shooting at protestors. Human chaos with absolute consequence was being revealed before me.

But my head was stuck in a game that had no nationality—a game that might as well have taken place in a Starbucks in Idaho. The following days were no different. When I and a few other reporters were speeding through a mist-blanketed marsh on an auto-rickshaw, the involuted vegetation reminded me of chess. During an interview with a kid who was shot through the wrist, I had to stifle the desire to ask him whether he was a chess player. And when I drank sweet hot tea in the evening rain near the Indian border, my mistaken moves were on my mind.

They were still there when I got back to Bangkok. I knew how badly I'd played, and I wanted to prove to myself that I could do better. Back at the apartment, I dropped my bag, pulled out my computer, and went to Chess.com to play a few online games. That became my night, which became my weekend.

Other tasks were accomplished, occasionally. Grudgingly, I completed the Nepal piece. It didn't turn out very well. Nothing else turned out very well. I could barely walk down the street to get my nightly meal of noodles at the corner noodle stand, because every important game of chess history is available for review on sites like Chessgames.com, and I was invariably staring at one of them on my phone when I was wandering the streets. This was the cause of a few near-death experiences, and more than a couple of collisions with other pedestrians.

I didn't care. I had simply forgotten how to care about anything else.

3

ONE NIGHT IN BANGKOK

My headlong descent into an Internet chess wormhole did terrible things to my personality. This is because Internet chess is a fertile breeding ground for hatred. When you're playing someone who isn't visible, known to you only by their nickname—SchellingFord or ButtSex69—your competitive instincts are unmitigated by the basic civilizing effect of the presence of a living person before you.

During one game, which had arrived at a complicated position, I spent ten minutes thinking about what moves I could make—which is not unusual. But my opponent typed, "You are slow delivery."

"Yes," I agreed.

"Play move."

"Don't feel like it."

"What cup size your mother?"

By the way, I should take a break from this riveting dialogue to mention that "a complicated position" is a configuration of the pieces in which it's hard to figure out whether a given move will create instant victory, instant death, or nothing at all. Along with the names of the openings, chess has a whole set of conventional phrases, which are fashioned from the linguistic habits of the great players of history. For example, you don't say "a great position"—you say "a pleasant position." Why? Because some Russian guy said it a long time ago, and now it's what *you* say, unless you want to sound uncivilized. It's like you would say you're having a "dirty martini" instead of a "salty martini."

But on the Internet, the patter is a little different. When somebody asks you what cup size your mother is, you say, "Fuck you."

"How your mother do it?"

I ignored his continuous abuse until right before the end of the game, when I offered the gracious message "You lose."

"Come in hell for cock suck," he responded.

My life was a constant alternation between triumph and ignominy, all delivered through the glow of my MacBook. The ratio of wins to losses was the determinant of my whole emotional spectrum. After a few back-to-back wins, I started thinking life was as sweet and easy as a gummy worm. But a long stretch of losses would infuse me with a feral anger. On those occasions, I went outside on the deck so I could scream at all the birds lining the trees behind the apartment.

These particular birds, which favored my neighborhood above all others, emitted a high whoop that sounded like the digitally distorted coo of a delighted child. Their cries were the punctuation of the early hours. They were chatty, too—when I called out to them, they shrieked right back. Slowly, while conversing with unseen animals, I recollected the chess knowledge I had lost in the previous decade.

At some point I became alarmed that I wasn't actively seeking human company. It wasn't exactly that I was getting lonelier. It's that I was disturbed by how little my loneliness was affecting me now that I was playing chess. This wasn't how I was supposed to be. It didn't measure up to the contemporary self-image I had painstakingly developed in Toronto. There was an ideal personality I was supposed to be striving for: that of a witty and urbane writer-type who would fling consequential phrases from his well-compensated fingers before going out in the evening to quip his way through intimate gatherings and win over strangers with lustrous anecdotes. But none of that was happening at all. In Bangkok, a bright and gritty city, totally free to be whomever I wanted, I was becoming a chess nerd.

So, I downloaded Tinder, in an attempt to prove to myself that I still possessed worldly desires. Resultantly, I met up with a cute girl named Sundae on a lantern-lit patio. She was charming and smart and full of contagious optimism, sure that both of our lives would be forever involved in a state of continuous improvement and joy. She laughed many times a minute as she excitedly talked in paragraphs. After dinner, she led me between bars playing horrible music that I moved to as if I knew how. We drank sour drinks that discomforted my organs. Before the end of the night, we were dancing pretty close. She kissed me and said she already missed me and then she hopped in a taxi. In the moment, she was exciting. But later that week, when she sent me a very felicitous text, I was deep in a chess game. I actually can't remember whether I responded at all, but if I did, my message probably wasn't compelling. Two days later, she texted me again, at 1 a.m., telling me that she had just redecorated her bedroom and now only needed someone who could admire it. But I didn't respond immediately, because I was deep in a chess game. I decided that maybe I'd text her back after the game was over. Or maybe after two. Or maybe I'd prefer to stay up all night, in the company of invisible opposition, rather than lie in the very visible arms of an attractive woman.

And as I pondered these options, it occurred to me that most of the behaviors displayed in my post-adolescent life—that whole urbane writer thing—could, by any diligent mind, be seen as the construction of a sexually marketable persona. Very consciously, I navigated away from being lonely and introverted, assuming that if I wrote some things that people liked, and put together an outfit or two, women would find me at least marginally interesting. This turned out to be a reasonable strategy, which I'd actually recommend to young men who like fiddling with synonyms. And yet, in that moment, I chose my laptop over Sundae. I didn't respond to her message, and she wisely didn't message me again.

My only contacts with non-chess reality were Elena and Sally, who provided me with a somewhat functional social life—sometimes I had rambling discussions about journalistic ethics with Sally, who ended up living in an apartment down the street, or went jogging through the smelly streets with Elena, dodging tuk-tuks and tourists and rat-infested trash piles. Sometimes they took me to parties and I even managed to make some halting conversation in between thoughts of the French Defense. But when Elena took a two-week vacation in Cambodia, and Sally got busy, life got dark. Hygiene became optional, then nonexistent. Lacking any responsibility, I went to sleep at 6 a.m. every night, watching the gelid early morning crawl across my filthy feet. Seventy percent of my diet was salty snacks in shiny bags. It got to a point where I realized that I was walking quickly around my apartment because I was fleeing my own smell.

Despite all my efforts, my virtuosity was not immediately forthcoming. In fact, I was barely making any improvement whatsoever. Partially, this is because I have a brain defect that makes chess difficult. Good chess play relies on visualization—picturing how the game will proceed once a few pieces are swapped around. Expert players are capable of playing blindfolded, following the game entirely through interior illustration. Some close their eyes when a game gets chaotic, preferring the mutability of their interior sketchpad over the intrusive object permanence that characterizes open-eyed life. Top-level elite players, in an outlandish example of cognitive specialization, often play multiple blindfolded games at once, painting many strategic mental pictures in parallel. Uzbek-American grandmaster Timur Gareyev, who isn't nearly the best player in the world with his eyes open, but who is weirdly good at blindfold chess, can play more than forty unsighted games at once.

But I am a sufferer of what's called aphantasia: the total lack of mental imagery. There are only words in my head; there are no pictures whatsoever. When I close my eyes and try to visualize a beach, I am trying to divide murky darkness into water and sand. My memories are film treatments. My former loves are concepts. So, while others picture bright lines and dancing dots when they're working on chess, I'm playing in the dark. Occasionally, I do attempt closed-eye calculation, but it's futile—nothing happens. I do it only out of a sense of longing, like how children attempt to fly by running around in circles and flapping their arms, hoping that gravity will depart at some moment, allowing their ascent.

Soon, my initially sluggish progress became completely stalled. And since chess was, at that moment, the only way I was measuring myself, my poor play made me sad, and then sadder. The spindly fingers of real despair began poking me in the head. Even toothpaste tasted a little bitter. Deep down, I started wondering whether I was worthless.

This was a sensation I knew well. Not just because of my childhood, but also because I've got another significant neural issue on top of aphantasia—bipolar disorder, which had rubbed my face in moods like this before, throughout my early twenties. Having had more than a few episodes, I'd become quite familiar with the stink of futility that lives right next door to suicidal thoughts. And, in turn, I knew that this darkness was often preceded by a period of ecstatic intellectual absorption. Over and over again, I'd become totally fascinated by something and dive into it until the fascination withered abruptly, at which point I'd start missing meals and thinking in a sort of low-key way about how I could maybe kill myself.

So, it occurred to me, in Bangkok, as I started feeling like a sack of fatback left under a heat lamp, that I might be in the middle of this cycle again. Perhaps my chess infatuation was just another vanishing fancy—another instance of my manic mind urging me to adopt an unlikely persona that would be discarded as soon as my self-loathing dictated that it should be.

But this wasn't supposed to happen, because a few years before I'd been placed on mood stabilizers, which had proven very effective. I hadn't had these feelings in a long time. So either chess had a unique power over my neurochemistry, or the powerful heat of Bangkok had been breaking down the active ingredients in my medication. To this day, I'm not sure which is more likely. I do wonder, now and again, how my life could've been different if I'd kept my pills in the fridge.

Regardless: I was becoming frightened of my increasingly hostile interior landscape, so I decided that I needed counsel. Therapy occurred to me, but I didn't know whether any clinician could fully grasp the importance of the French Defense. Instead, I decided I needed the presence of other chess players, who would steer me in the right direction. I took a shower, got on the Skytrain, and went to meet the Bangkok Chess Club.

The club met on the upper floor of a pub on the far end of Soi Cowboy, one of Bangkok's high-efficiency sex markets. Pink lights illuminated pink banners over bars where pink drinks were served by women wearing pink bikinis. Reality was painted one color. Up and down the neon-coated avenue, the working women preened with numbers pinned to their chests. It was a slow night, so the salesmanship was particularly energetic. One woman in a barely existing spandex onesie took my hand and asked me where I was going. When I didn't offer a distinct answer, she took hold of my crotch. I gently removed her hand from my person, saying something like, "Excuse me, ma'am, I have to go to chess club."

You might have a stereotyped conception of what a chess club looks like. You might imagine that club players tend towards the bespectacled, the dramatically ectomorphic, and the pimpled. You might envision yawning holes in shirts worn by men with improperly thriving facial hair.

You would be correct. There are, in fact, some pretty hot chess masters—if you're inclined towards verifying this statement, do a google of Robin van Kampen and/or Sopiko Guramishvili—but chess doesn't, I think, tend to attract the attractive. After all, chess is a sport that rewards seclusion. To be any good at all, you have to spend a lot of time study- ing. And to really be great, you have to wrap your mind around the Database—the fearsome database of all chess possibility.

See, one fact about the game that seems like a basic for- mality but is actually tremendously consequential is that every move of every serious game is recorded. Every time you put down a piece, you write down what you did on a scorecard. Your opponent does, too, for the sake of con- sensus, and then somebody—a tournament organizer, or whoever—types in the moves and puts the game online. In this way, the great mosaic—the Database—is formed. It's big. To give you an idea, ChessBase, the main chess database company, includes eight million games in its Mega Database. And that eight million is a teensy slice of all the games ever recorded. It's just the essential stuff, the games that a grand- master might want to look at. After all, you can't leave home without knowing what ten thousand people have done with the Botvinnik Variation of the Semi-Slav Defense.

Also, like religious scripture, the important games are annotated by the game's luminaries, and then the annotations are annotated. This mass of commentary is included in the Database, too, and thus chess lovers converse with each other across the decades, discovering the truth of chess through the investigation of its minute details. Players who don't spend time absorbing this conversation are less armed than those who do, meaning that they can't attain the heights of the game.

If you're pretty, there are more easily obtainable joys. So there's a sort of brain drain—some would say a reverse brain drain—of the gorgeous away from the ranks of players. Accordingly, as I climbed to the second floor of the pub, I found a group of homely people clustered around a dozen boards—geeky Thais of all ages, a clutch of Bangladeshi adolescents, and paunchy English retirees whose hands were always around a beer.

I found the unloveliness lovely. While, as I've mentioned previously, I'd figured out how to modify my behavior so I could hang out with pretty artist types, I'd also long felt unsure about the worth of this masquerade—I often found it more tiring than fulfilling. You've got to be conversant in the latest of both conceptual art and R & B. Your clothing has to be nice but not too nice. You've got to air the required progressive platitudes whenever a remotely political subject comes up. And so on, and so on.

At chess club, there's none of that. Social affiliation has

only one cost: the game of chess. Friendship in chess is simple. It isn't about smartly signaling that you've got the right opinions about recent topics. It's about examining small areas of the game's infinite tapestry—finding each other in a landscape that transcends the complexities of cultural taste, as well as every geographical boundary. This common bond engenders a positive spirit. With the exception of a few petty jerks, chess players tend to be cooperative creatures.

True to this tendency, I was given a warm welcome by a player named Mike after he saw me wander in with a confused look on my face. He was one of those wiry little men who seemed like he'd be handy in a hypothetical knife fight. He also wore a knife holster on his calf. He suggested we play a casual game. "I'm not very good," I told him. "I'm just okay," he said, "don't worry." As it quickly turned out, his "just okay" was more than okay enough for me. He smiled as he captured my pieces with the joy of a child advancing on a butterscotch. His concentration was absolute—his tiny eyes spun in their sockets as his pupils conversed with every square on the board. We played what's referred to as "blitz": games where each player must make all their moves in no more than five minutes total. After a bit of blitz, it was determined that I wasn't adequate competition.

Looking for a more suitable matchup, he paired me with Jim, a player who was mildly intoxicated after one drink, which impelled him to brag loudly about being very drunk. He was, in other words, eighteen—a spindly guy with a grating, somewhat rodential voice. "You will be a good challenge," he said, then beat me in two blitz games.

"You suck at fast chess," he said, "let's play slow." He dialed back the timer, giving us each fifteen minutes. This added thinking time gave me a huge advantage. I started seeing flaws in the sloppy excitability that was the essential feature of his style. In response, he became steelier, and spoke without apparent self-consciousness or innuendo about wanting to "grind" in the "holes" in my position. "I want that hole," he said, pointing to a gap in my pawns where his knight might nestle.

"You should enter the tournament," he said, during our last game. "When you're not playing like a dickhead, you're not bad. You could learn something by being crushed by a grandmaster." He was referring to the fact that the upcoming tournament, the Bangkok Open, was, as the name indicated, an open tournament, where any lonely essayist could play alongside real competition—experienced veterans or very young chess assassins practically suckled on the game's classic offensive maneuvers. Previously, playing in the tournament had seemed like a preposterous idea. I'd seen it advertised on the club's Facebook group, but I hadn't seriously considered entering. But Jim's retainer-contained smile was strangely convincing. Following his backhanded compliment, I checkmated him with a flashy piece sacrifice—a sequence in which I allowed the capture of one of my rooks but undid his position by waltzing through the resulting chaos. "I guess you're right," I said, as I cornered his king. "I guess I'm not as bad as I thought."

"Strong finish, very strong," said Mike, who was quietly watching over my shoulder. Seeing that I was, in fact, capable of not playing like a dickhead, he rejoined our company. "We both play the French Defense," he said. "What lines do you like?" Until the bar closed, we engaged in fervent debates about our favorite positions.

"You have some potential," he said, "some of your moves are very good. You just don't have confidence in yourself. You play like a weak man. You are not a weak man. You are not fast, but you have the power of intelligence." He told me to call him Teacher Mike, then gave me his phone number, in case I wanted to meet up for a chess hang. He gave me an unexpectedly earnest hug, his nose landing right between my pecs. I filled out the tournament forms as soon as I got home.

■■■

That first night at chess club brought me back from the edge of melancholy. The presence of a purpose—a potential victory at the Bangkok Open—changed everything. Even though I was still suffering many painful losses, the pain presented itself as the cost of striving, rather than as simple punishment. I was fighting a hard battle, instead of just incurring damage, as I had been before. I studied hard every day and went to the club weekly, sponging up all the wisdom I could from Teacher Mike. But in spite of my improved mood and my renewed dedication, my self-administered education was still somewhat ineffectual. My relationship with chess was still in a stage characterized by lust and terror. The game's breadth both wowed and dismayed me. I felt tiny in its grasp. And, lost as I was, I couldn't figure out what kind of player I wanted to be.

There are different kinds of players, and broadly, you can sort them by how crazy they are. Some players, like Vladimir Fedoseev, are all about bloodthirsty verve, preferring complicated struggles that end with a dramatic demise, whether theirs or their opponents'. They're here for a good time, not for a long time. Others, like Dutch wunderkind Anish Giri, are brooding rationalists, engaged in an unhurried hunt for a series of small advantages that might, together, ensure domination.

But beyond that, there's a world of individual quirks, like those belonging to my favorite player, the brilliant and beloved Vassily Ivanchuk, otherwise known as "Chucky," a fearful opponent who tends to wear either beautifully tailored formalwear or bright pink Adidas tracksuits. His lovability stems from an unlikely combination of inhuman genius and an all-too-human inconsistency. Depending on the day of the week, he plays either like Prometheus, capable of making World Champions cry, or like a bumbling nincompoop, capable of losing seven games in a row to inferior opposition. At his best, his moves seem incomprehensible—awkward maneuvers and seemingly dubious tactical thrusts—but they reveal themselves to be part of an unconventional plan that ends in your seemingly unavoidable demise.

That's how I wanted to play, I'd decide, for a day or two. I wanted to be complicated and idiosyncratic. But soon I'd completely reverse that decision, assuring myself that I should adopt a resolute, defensive style, a shift that would then last a couple of days until I changed my ways once again. Now, looking back, this inconstancy seems impossibly silly. I was like a child who couldn't draw a house with crayons deciding whether to be more like Jackson Pollock or Francis Bacon. But that's where I was at—wheeling around wildly, gaining little.

It's worth noting briefly that I was still writing some essays for money, but they didn't make much of an impact on me, or probably on anyone who read them once they were released. The work felt as perfunctory as grooming. The only real non-chess thing that I paid attention to was sesame soy milk, which was the foundation of my diet during this time. Every day, I really miss sesame soy milk—the fact that it's generally unavailable in North America is probably why we have so much violent crime. Homicidal people all over the Americas, when dealing with runaway emotions, drink Coca-Cola, which inflames their already chaotic emotions with its corrosive acidity and carbonation. But there's another possible world, where the maniacs who commit gruesome atrocities are swaddled in the felicitously innocuous flavor of thick, khaki-colored sesame soy milk. Available in any 7-Eleven in Bangkok.

Strangely, I now remember those pre-tournament days fondly, and not just because of the specialty beverages of Southeast Asia. When you're devoting your life to chess, even if the devotion is as troubled as mine was, there's a satisfying purity to it all. You're surrendering yourself to a search for aesthetic pleasure as well as mental fitness. Chess, to the seasoned player, is pretty like poetry is pretty—it bears the wonder of indelible combinations arising from a simple language. Just as how phrases like "fuck you" or "pass the salt" use the same language as phrases like "Time held me green and dying, though I sang in my chains like the sea," the rules of chess are simple, but the combinations they yield are ecstatically various. And, just like a line of Dylan Thomas inflicts elation on a poetry lover, the surprises that are revealed across the board unleash little quanta of delight in the chess player's heart.

This monomania created a significant temporal distortion. The week before the tournament seemed to go by in seconds. And when the fateful morning arrived, I awoke tired, barely roused from a half-sleep, feeling as human as a gum wrapper. The sky was empty of clouds, the sun blared as ever, and the anxiety was incredible. I would have told you, that morning, that this was my first real test on earth. Every other standard by which I'd been measured was bankrupt—including, and especially, the opinions of my loved ones. People are easily fooled, after all. They can't tell how corrupt you really are—they don't know about your disgusting thoughts or your impure intentions. But chess can't be charmed. You can't fake chess.

My emotional state swung between various extremities, never quite cohering. Leaving my apartment, I was shot through with an incandescent cockiness—I was sure, at the end of the commute, that I would utterly bulldoze my unfortunate opponent. My hubris was such that I dreamt of what I'd do with the prize money. It was about three thousand Canadian dollars—enough, I figured, for a half-dozen Michelin-starred meals in Paris with a ravishing date. But by the time I got off the Skytrain, the excitement had turned toxic—my stomach was in the process of violently rejecting my coffee. There was a taste of nascent vomit in my mouth. My inner life was entirely consumed by a high, pure sense of terror. I couldn't recall any of the opening theory I had painstakingly studied. When I went looking in my memory, I could recall only that bishops move diagonally.

The tournament was held in a giant ballroom at a fancy-ish hotel. I got there three hours early. An insipid bossa nova trio was playing "Hey Jude," slightly fudging the lyrics—the singer sang "Hey dude" instead of "Hey Jude," which was all right with me. I bought a sandwich, and then, suddenly skeptical about the whole concept of ingestion, threw it out. The whole morning went by in this fashion—me doing nothing, quietly losing my shit.

As the players filed in, Teacher Mike greeted me in the lobby.

"I'll be watching you," he said.

"Do you have any advice?" I asked.

"Be calm," he said. "Ignore psychology, ignore yourself, ignore the face of your opponent—just play a good move."

His advice was sound, but following it was far beyond my capability. I was slipping into the kind of full panic in which my physical coordinates were somewhat mysterious to my conscious mind, and time became unaccountable. Somehow, as if placed there by a fastidious tornado, I was sitting at one table among many, alongside a placard bearing my name, with a slot accommodating a small tabletop Canadian flag, upon which I wiped my forehead.

My opponent was a friendly Scot named Joseph Diaphragm.

Okay, that actually wasn't his name. But, as my publisher's trusty lawyer told me, my opponents could sue me if they claim I've depicted them dishonestly and/or unflatteringly. So I've given them extremely realistic alternate names, like Joseph Diaphragm, as a way of protecting their identities.

We chatted amiably before the game began. I could barely listen—the noise inside my head muted his speech.

"I'm a reporter who can't play chess," I said.

"I work on submarines," he said.

"So you'll cry deep underwater if I beat you," I said.

"I suppose so."

"You won't be crying, though."

"Why do you say that?"

"Well, I'm an unrated player."

A note on ratings: every player registered with FIDE, the world chess federation, is given a numerical grade upon which their happiness depends entirely. It's an instant read on where you are in the chess food chain. Cuppies like me—semi-promising amateurs—are usually putzing around somewhere between 1200 and 1900. Elite players weigh in above 2500, the minimum score required for a shot at the "grandmaster" title—the highest existing designation of chess office. Beyond even that enviable plateau lies the less formally defined realm of the "super-grandmaster"— we're talking about players beyond 2700, like current World Champion Magnus Carlsen, peak rating 2882.

Every time you win, lose, or draw a game, your score is adjusted based on an equation that determines whether you've performed at, above, or below a level that could be expected of a player of your current rating. This means that if a grandmaster defeats a low-rated player, their rating might not be adjusted at all, but if the reverse happens, a tremendous transfer of rating points will take place, since the former result would be an entirely expected event, and the latter result would be an astounding coup.

"What's your rating?" is almost a rude question among amateur players, because the subject is taken so seriously—desperate tears are often wept about losing a dozen rating points through a casual blunder. For anyone other than a confident chess professional, it's a question as probing as "What's your relationship with God?" or "Do you feel insecure about your sexual performance?" Basically, unless you're one of the best players on the planet, your rating is a measure of your dreams' distance.

Joseph was rated about 2092—a shade short of a master. This made a victory against him unlikely. But not impossible.

"Unrated players are kind of scary," he said. "You might secretly be very good."

GAME 1 JOSEPH DIAPHRAGM VS. SASHA CHAPIN

The air was hard, slippery glass in my lungs. I had worn a charcoal suit in which I was cooking, lobster-like. This sartorial choice was made in accordance with a notice I'd seen which said that players should dress in proper attire. But upon seeing the other players, I realized that I'd misinterpreted this guideline. The general state of the outfits in the room suggested that, in this case, "proper attire" meant that players should avoid wearing anything sludge-covered, ripped, or fully transparent, not that players should wear formalwear, as I was. As the games began, I felt microwaved. The tournament director announced the beginning of the round, the entire room shook hands at once, and all sound died away except for the quiet clacks of the clocks. Before me, on the board, a position was taking shape.

My dread, previously ferocious, instantly multiplied. I felt like I was gazing into the Void.

My own personal conception of existential dread is idiosyncratic. Many people, I think, are troubled by their own insignificance, preferring not to think about being a tiny part of a vanishing species in what couldn't even be called a corner of the galaxy. Not me—I'm fine with that. Moreover, I'm not perturbed by the fact that I'll be remembered by very few of the 108 billion people who have ever lived. Yes: I'm a standard-model dude in an endless something or other. It's mostly fine. Endlessness is easily understood, easily labeled with a three-syllable word, placed in the dictionary beside equally simple concepts like *enchilada*. Infinity itself escapes experience, but the notion is a short phrase—it just doesn't stop. That's all infinity does, or rather doesn't do. It doesn't scare me.

What does scare me—what provokes real horror in me—is my lack of understanding. I see mental horror— the Void—in the tumbling numbers of securities trading, or the heaps of barely decipherable ancient papyrus dug up in the Middle East, or the global weather patterns that have evaded, to this date, capture by any mathematical model. I am troubled by the world's great throngs of data—by thickets of facts I might comprehend individually, but that together make a chaos capable of receding before me as long as I live.

That's what I felt, staring at the board in front of me. I was terrified by the profusion of possible moves offered by my pieces. Normally, even if I was playing terribly, each terrible move was the extension of a certain kind of logic—the game was comprehensible. But, in that moment, nothing was comprehensible. I felt like I couldn't put my pieces anywhere, because I felt like I could put them everywhere, for all eternity. I essentially blacked out. My hand made moves with the assistance of my arm, while my eyes helplessly beheld their work. And, on my scorecard, I made marks that were indecipherable even by me.

I lost the game in fifteen moves, in fifteen minutes—an astonishingly brief amount of time, considering that tournament games usually last around four hours. My incompetence was outstanding. I played worse than I ever had. Calmly, I maneuvered into the Queen's Gambit Declined Defense, a safe option I usually enjoyed playing, then gave one of my rooks away for no reason at all. I began laughing a crazy, red-faced laugh. A tournament official threatened to eject me if I didn't quiet down.

"I think I should give up," I told Diaphragm, in a desperate and brief bid for some sympathy, in violation of the rule that players aren't allowed to talk during tournament games other than to offer a draw or resign.

"Really?"

"Well, it's basically over."

"It's completely up to you."

"Maybe I'll play on."

"Good."

I made another move. He nodded, then took the other piece I had just given him.

"I resign," I said.

"Very well," he said.

We shook hands.

"Would you like to analyze the game?" he said.

This is a nice part of chess tradition. Upon finishing a game, etiquette dictates that the players should at least briefly examine what's occurred. You review the best moves, point out opportunities your opponent may have missed, and generally come to a conclusion about what kind of game you just had—an even struggle, a boring stalemate, or a clumsy brawl. When two grandmasters do this, it's somewhat like two supercomputers having a jocular conversation. Multiplicative strings of calculation spill out from smiling faces, delivered with the giddy sing-song of fanatics dwelling on their favorite subject. But Diaphragm was asking me whether I'd enjoy teasing out the subtleties of a blunt massacre that could've been inflicted on my unbelievably bad play by a competent six-year-old.

"No, thanks," I said.

"Don't worry," he said, "it's just the first game."

"Yeah," I said, "the first game."

I left the hotel. All I can say about the rest of the day is that it occurred. Probably I ate noodles, like I always did. Perhaps I breathed heavily, wondering what would become of me. Noticing a light blinking at the top of a distant skyscraper seems within the realm of possibility. Really I can't tell you.

After I slept for twelve hours, I emailed the tournament directors, announcing my resignation. I would not be attending the remaining six games. This brought me great, instant relief. Clearly, I had been right when I was a teenager—chess just wasn't my game. A chess hobby would lead only to misery and frustration. I decided to quit, and to keep doing things I was good at.

My tourist visa expired immediately after the tournament. In a few days, it would be illegal for me to remain in Thailand. This was a little sad, but I figured it was about the right time to leave. While Bangkok is a city that makes most other places seem hopelessly boring, I was starting to miss the concerns of home—all the politics and fashions and acquaintanceships. They'd seemed like nothing but deluding fluff when I left Toronto, but I realized that without all that stuff, it's hard to know what life is about, unless you're obsessed with chess, which wasn't the plan anymore.

So I booked a flight for New York City, where I planned to spend a short, expensive period of time before returning home. I had farewell noodles with Elena and Sally, packed my few possessions, and got on a plane. And my mind was clear and my heart was easy. Slipping through the clouds, I felt the lives I'd thought I would live peeling away. As I recalled all the people I'd met in Thailand, I briefly thought of my allies at the Bangkok Chess Club, who might wonder where I'd gone. But that didn't really matter. Any thoughts of me would be replaced by speculations about the Berlin Defense.

Regardless, I would soon be in Brooklyn, surrounded by old friends, beautiful strangers, and deli sandwiches— matters much more consequential than a rook maneuver. I happily vowed that my life as a chess player was over.

4

A PUZZLE WITHOUT A SOLUTION

There are those moments when you're aware that your human programming is a little defective. You become acquainted with the possibility that you've been designed to pursue insane commitments directly opposed to your survival. In these moments, when you feel like you need to call God on His private line and demand a refund for what He personally placed in your cranial cavity, it's sometimes reassuring to remember that you're probably not alone. Given the number of people who have lived and died, there's usually someone, alive or otherwise, whose faults resemble your own. For this reason, I often seek consolation in the story of Marcel Duchamp, a man whose chess problem was a lot like mine, but dialed up to an implausible intensity.

You probably know Duchamp's work, or have at least heard of him. Duchamp is considered one of the most important artists of the twentieth century, a reputation he established by infuriating people. First, he did it with the widely mocked painting *Nude Descending a Staircase, No. 2*, which consists of a jangling mass of shapes only vaguely suggesting a human figure doing anything at all. Then, he tried to get a urinal displayed at a major art exhibition, declaring that it was an artwork simply because of that declaration, a move rejected even by many of his artsiest peers.

Duchamp is both loved and loathed—celebrated as the man who freed artists from their old constraints, and vilified by the people who thought those constraints were a good idea. Maybe one time you went to an art gallery, and there was a bunch of stuff smeared on one wall and a pile of junk a few feet away, and you wondered where the art was. Stuff like that is partly Duchamp's fault.

What's not as well known about Marcel Duchamp is that, by the age of thirty-one, he had basically abandoned art in favor of chess.

This was just a spectacularly weird decision. In his twenties, Duchamp lived the most ravishing possible version of an artist's life. His every day was boozy and carefree. He was the toast of an intellectual coterie, and his many lovers came and went. He didn't even pay rent—a rich family took care of his accommodation in exchange for future artwork. And his few expenses were paid for by occasional French lessons he gave, by all accounts semi-competently, which were attended mostly by a gaggle of female admirers. And, although he wasn't yet famous outside the elite New York art scene, his reputation was expanding.

So, in fact, he lived the kind of life I supposedly wanted before my adult infatuation with chess. He was a celebrity to a very specific demographic, and enjoyed a fantastic love life as a result. His eccentricities were regarded with fascination and rewarded with cash. He was doing well out there, in the non-chess arena.

But chess, which he was introduced to as an adolescent, slowly encroached on his imagination, just as it did mine. More and more, throughout his early adulthood, he was seen at a chessboard, even during parties, where he checkmated his colleagues rather than engaging in flirtation or regular whiskey talk. As his twenties drew to a close, he spent almost every evening at New York's famous Marshall Chess Club. And after the age of thirty, although he wrote about (and sold reproductions of) his earlier work, there wasn't much art going on. It took him a decade to complete his second-last major piece, *The Large Glass,* mostly because he was bored of art and preferred chess. After that, he produced exactly one sculpture. Eventually, he came to feel that chess was a nobler pursuit than art. In a 1952 interview with *Time* magazine, he said, "It has all the beauty of art—and much more. It cannot be commercialized. Chess is much purer than art in its social position."

It makes sense that Duchamp, specifically, felt this way.

His work, in part, was about saying "fuck you" to grand, stuffy pieties about what art was. One of his most famous works was a defacement of the *Mona Lisa:* on a postcard reproduction of the original painting, he gave her a moustache and framed her with the letters LHOOQ, which, if read aloud in French, sound like the phrase "she has a hot ass." This, as well as the infamous aforementioned urinal, were part of a series of "readymades"—mundane objects he treated as sacred artifacts. Together, these works seemingly displayed an exasperation with the dishonest pageantry of the role of art in society. They formed a serious rebellion against self-seriousness.

But in chess, of course, there is no pageantry—none of the pompousness that Duchamp's work tried to skewer. One can't speculate about whether a chess move is honest or dishonest. Chess can't be pretentious, or self-serious. It's just not that kind of thing. It's simpler than all of that. It is what it is.

This was one part of my many-limbed fixation, as well. Being the kind of writer I am—a memoirist, I guess—has always struck me as a little sad, because it means that I'm constantly wondering whether any definable portion of my experience is marketable. I'm forever observing myself from a mercantile perspective, noting whether any of my minor melancholies or brief discomposures might be salable. Essentially, I'm a parasite on my own life. Any compelling character I meet excites me not only because they're exciting but also because I might describe them profitably. If I met you, I'd probably wonder how I'd condense your characteristics if I needed to put you in an essay.

It just seems better out there in Chessland. Better than what I do. Better than constantly pawing at whatever occurs around me, whatever romance or dilemma, and thinking, "Maybe this could be a titillating paragraph." Like Duchamp, I'm not entirely convinced of the validity of my profession.

Duchamp's favorite thing, even more than playing in tournaments, was solving chess puzzles. Puzzles are how players stay sharp. You're given a position where one side has one winning move, which, if it's a good puzzle, is between difficult and impossible to find. All you know is the puzzle's main instruction, something like "White to play and win." By solving a lot of puzzles, you absorb tactical patterns that might emerge during play, so that, if they arise on the board during competition, you'll recognize them even though you're freaking out. They're target practice, as well as a stress-free way of exploring the game's possibilities. Duchamp conducted such explorations basically all the time, rising at noon after staring at chess positions until the early hours.

The natural expectation is that Duchamp, intelligent as he was, would become a great chess player, given that he loved the game so much and was so dedicated. And I'd like to tell you that he did, because that would be a lovely story of a man remaking himself through sheer will—a tale of perseverance being rewarded. Ideally, after years of forsaking companionship, money, and fame, Duchamp would've emerged transformed.

Unfortunately, that's not the case. Duchamp got pretty good after a decade's intense focus—better than me, certainly—but he was never excellent. At his peak, he was just skilled enough to win some small-potatoes regional tournaments. (This was easier to do in the early twentieth century than it is now, in that chess was a less populated and less studied sport.) And although he was an incredibly inventive artist, he wasn't a very inventive player. He didn't leave behind an opening variation of his own, or any novel maneuvers—there's no Duchamp Attack, or anything like that.

In the final analysis, Duchamp gave up being one of the great shit-stirrers of the artistic tradition, and ended up being a mild curiosity in the history of chess. He knew this, but he couldn't stop. His obsession was such that it ended his only marriage, to Lydie Sarazin-Levassor, who had to put up with Duchamp's spending every day of their honeymoon in Nice at the local chess club. Before their marriage dissolved—it lasted six months—she glued his chess set's every piece to its board, a drastic step that proved entirely futile. "I am still a victim of chess," he said, in the aforementioned *Time* magazine interview.

The only significant contribution that Duchamp made to the chess literature was a puzzle he composed himself.

It's a weird puzzle, in that it doesn't look very puzzle-like, which is to say, it doesn't seem like a position that might yield a dramatic conclusion. It looks like a totally standard situation: it's a rook and pawn endgame, a typical final stage of a drawn-out battle, where only rooks, pawns, and kings remain on the board. To the experienced student's eye, it looks like a draw. Many rook and pawn endgames can't be won by either side, if both play correctly: the rooks march around each other endlessly, sweeping away the pawns, barring the kings from doing anything decisive. In other words, Duchamp's puzzle seems like it has no solution.

This is because it doesn't. Give the position to a chess engine and it'll tell you that you're looking at a drawn game. Duchamp was an advanced enough player that he surely knew this: that although the white player possessed a pawn dangerously poised a square away from becoming a queen, the black player was entirely capable of preventing its metamorphosis. One can only conclude that the puzzle was a symbol of what chess, as a whole, meant to Duchamp: an intoxicating frustration.

It's not Duchamp's fault that he was never that good. First of all, he was just too late. As is true of me, his period of intense study began in his twenties rather than his infancy, which is really where it has to begin if you plan on becoming competitive. Greatness requires an early acquaintance with the game's classic patterns—a basic education delivered long before the first whispers of pubescence. If you're an adult learner, your brain is too old and rigid for the deep neural adaptation you need. Chess demands the sole ownership of a bunch of brain cells that the post-adolescent mind may have already devoted to the ability to navigate a grocery store lineup without screaming, or, in Duchamp's case, the social aptitude required to deal with the more irritating members of his milieu. If you're a player starting late in life, the most you can be, generally, is third class. Duchamp actually did remarkably well, given the low ceiling of chess achievement available to a late bloomer.

Moreover, age isn't the only factor that constrained Duchamp's success. If that were the sole determinant of chess mastery, then every intelligent player who started young and had a solid work ethic would have a shot at the World Championship. But that's not the case. That's really, really not the case. Being great at chess is also a matter of raw talent. Chess is one of those things, like music or math, that certain minds really fuse with. You just have it, or you don't.

I feel like I need to defend this statement with some hard data, since the very concept of talent has gone out of style. It's unfashionable to claim that people are exceptional, in any domain, because of any intrinsic gifts. It's more often claimed that variations in ability are mostly or exclusively based on varying amounts of deliberate practice. Mastery, supposedly, is just a matter of working hard—you could be a master, too, with the right level of dedication. Over the last decade or so, this position has been expounded by many, many authors. Probably the most notable advocate is Malcolm Gladwell, whose book *Outliers* popularized the now-famous "10,000-Hour Rule": if you're really good at something, it's because you've spent about ten thousand hours on it.

Now, obviously, nobody is silly enough to think that talent doesn't exist, period. That's not the debate here. The existence of talent is proven by the fact of people like Srinivasa Ramanujan—the man who, without any formal training, became one of the greatest mathematicians who ever lived, effortlessly emitting utterly complicated theorems that astounded his colleagues. The debate here is about proportion. It's about whether people like Ramanujan, the true freaks, are the only cases in which talent is a primary factor—whether talent is relevant only in the most extreme cases. Can we ordinary people blame talent for our lack of success? When we say that we don't have talent, are we just coming up with a convenient excuse for our lack of diligence? To what extent can we transcend certain inborn aptitudes?

These are big questions. They don't have simple answers, or at least none that I'm qualified to provide. But if we limit the discussion to chess, the answer is clear. The data shows that talent matters. A lot.

Probably the most persuasive piece of evidence that talent is important in games in general is a meta-analysis conducted by Macnamara et al., published in *Psychological Science* in 2014. After analyzing a combination of eighty-eight studies of skill acquisition, the researchers concluded that, when it comes to games, only 26 percent of individual variance in skill level can be attributed to practice. Practice is valuable, but its importance is dominated by a combination of other factors, like working memory, general intelligence, and starting age. So the paper suggests that if you want to be a world-class player, you should start really, really young and be really, really lucky with your genetics. This was further corroborated by another meta-analysis conducted by the same researchers, pertaining specifically to chess players, which demonstrated the same conclusion.

Now, there's an obvious objection here—can't playing chess make you more intelligent, thus improving your raw talent in a roundabout way? Well, current evidence says no. According to another study published in *Current Directions in Psychological Science,* playing chess doesn't improve your non-chess faculties significantly. (One interesting implication here is that a lot of the chess economy is built on a fraud: lots of parents send their children to expensive chess camps in an effort to make them smarter, in the same way that some other parents enhance their babies with Mozart, but this effort seems futile, based on the data.)

This is not nearly all of the evidence for my side of the debate. There are a lot more factors that make the deliberate practice hypothesis look even more doomed. Like the fact that the ability to practice for hours is itself genetically influenced—it relies on traits like conscientiousness, which are highly heritable. But we don't need to explore that too deeply. The basic case is made: talent matters. Unless all of this research somehow fails to replicate, or is fundamentally flawed in non-obvious ways—which, of course, is possible— then Gladwell's rule does not belong on the chessboard.

So, then, exactly how big is the gulf between the talented player and the untalented player? Quite simply: it's huge.

One way of demonstrating this is by producing some anecdotes about the sheer intellectual freakishness of the greatest players, like Bobby Fischer. Fischer's brain was odd. My favorite example of what I mean goes as follows. In 1972, Fischer was hanging around Reykjavik for a few days before playing the World Championship there. He called a friend of his, whose daughter answered the phone and told him in Icelandic that her father was away. Fischer didn't know a word of Icelandic, and so hung up the phone. The next day, he mentioned the call to an Icelandic chess player, and repeated, syllable for syllable, what the little girl had said to him, accurately enough that the Icelandic player was able to understand it. If this is how easily Fischer's mind could hang on to a jumble of phonemes drawn from a difficult foreign language, one could imagine how ably his mind could manipulate the minutiae of his favorite game.

We could also dwell, for a moment, upon a more direct demonstration of the freakishness of great players—the chess phenomenon called the simultaneous exhibition, or "simul." (Rhymes with "primal.") Simuls are events where a high-rated player plays a large number of parallel games with lower-rated players at the same time. They're a theatrical manifestation of the true depth of chess mastery. It's the chess equivalent of those scenes in a martial arts movie where Jackie Chan effortlessly defeats two dozen opponents with an attitude of zesty bonhomie.

But in simuls, there are often more than two dozen opponents, especially if you're Magnus Carlsen, the current World Champion, perhaps the greatest player to have ever lived. In February 2016, Magnus played a seventy-board simul in Hamburg. That's him versus seventy competent amateur players, at once.

Think about that. Think about a giant playing hall, filled with seventy players like me, who deeply love the game of chess and who have, like Duchamp, put in years of devotion and sacrifice. They've forsaken summer afternoons, and warm embraces, and a knowledge of the wider world, so that they might achieve greatness in an art which will never be appreciated by most people alive. And, in return for their fanaticism, they've earned the honor of facing the greatest breathing player. For each and every one, this is an Important Life Occasion, and they commit every available bit of brain bandwidth to making as perfect a move as possible, every move. They love Magnus, but in that span of six hours, their love is replaced by an adversarial froth. Each considers their game a matter of the utmost significance, and hopes this might be the hour of their greatest work.

On the other hand, Magnus, looking cool and trim as always, is strolling from board to board, thinking, "Hmm, that move looks good," and making it, after only a brief moment of contemplation. During each of those brief moments, immensely complicated calculations are made, at frightening speed, by the highly trained chess-related machinery that lurks behind his skull. He's one of those people who looks at the board and just sees, without effort, the game's distant horizons—a shimmering array of what could be. Variations flutter out before him, as clear as the branches of a bare tree. And this calculating power is enhanced by an unusually deep memory, a memory that has fully absorbed thousands and thousands of games, both notable brilliancies and trivial squabbles. Every time he looks at pieces on a board, their positions are automatically compared with the position of every piece in every game he's ever played, and the plethora of games he's ever studied, as well as patterns absorbed from tens of thousands of puzzles. The result of this combination of preternatural aptitude and slavish training is an eerie, near-perfect intuition. With seemingly little effort, in seconds, Magnus finds moves that lesser players would never dream of, even if given days of cogitation time.

Magnus won sixty-nine of those seventy simultaneous games. One of them was a draw. The player who drew him will treasure, for the rest of his life, that he held off one-seventieth of Magnus's skill. That's how good great chess players are. That's how wide the gap is.

And Magnus is actually infamous for not needing to study quite as hard as other high-level players. He makes sure to live a well-rounded life, avoiding the stereotypical monasticism of figures like Bobby Fischer. He plays soccer, has a well-documented beautiful girlfriend, and is an occasional fashion model—like me, he kind of looks like a low-budget version of Matt Damon. He prepared for his first game with Garry Kasparov, a former World Champion, by reading comics rather than reviewing his openings, having faith that his mind was robust enough that he didn't need to do any last-minute cramming. He was twelve. The game was a draw. Talent matters.

This is bittersweet news for the aspiring player. On the one hand, you're basically relegated by your genetics to a certain valley of the chess landscape, and you find out where you are only after you've labored for a number of years, when you either dwarf your peers or vice versa. On the other hand, this means that you can't hate yourself for not being a great player. It's not fair, any more than it would be fair for nearsighted people to lambaste themselves for not piloting fighter jets. It just doesn't make sense. Unless you're some kind of maniac, you should be satisfied by what small improvements you can make.

But maybe you are some kind of maniac. Maybe you're a fantastically arrogant person who loves chess but can't accept that you're not great at it. Perhaps the joy of playing your favorite game is matched by the constant pain of knowing how badly you're playing it, such that every game you play is like vigorously stabbing yourself with your favorite knife. Perhaps this mix of elation and loathing produces a deep and sorrowful addiction, such that you're spending almost literally all of your time on chess, even though it doesn't necessarily make you happy. And seeing yourself trapped in this vicious cycle, you vow to quit, because you'd like to be able to do normal things like have a job and a girlfriend and stuff, rather than hang out with a board game on your laptop every night. But, regardless of how earnestly you make this vow, your conviction is immediately slain by the force of your compulsion. As Omar Khayyam once wrote, "Indeed, indeed, repentance oft before I swore—but was I sober when I swore?"

That was me, in May, having returned from Bangkok.

After a brief, pleasant vacation in New York, I arrived in Toronto and took a room that smelled like sauerkraut above a crowded street whose people I spied on, feeling resentful and insecure. For the last five months I had been "traveling," which is a fun substitute for an identity. Now I wasn't sure what sort of person I was planning on being. All around me in the waking springtime I saw people coming alive, breezing through the intersection in flamboyant outfits, and wondered how they were pulling it off.

My time away left me with no real insights. My worldview was not transformed.

Everything was essentially unmodified, including me. While I wasn't sure what I expected, I was sure that it hadn't happened. Maybe the phrase "run away to find yourself" is so common because it's hard to find anything else. You don't necessarily accumulate profound knowledge. You simply see what pants are in fashion in a different time zone. You drink different beer, but the sun is the same and so are you. Then, you leave.

The only thing that was different about me was, well, chess. Or, rather, at that point, the lack of chess, because I'd sworn to give it up—both to myself and to the few friends who knew about the more tedious details of my existence. After all, life was out there for the taking, and I shouldn't spend all my time getting checkmated. But there was a cavity in my head where all the churning about the Poisoned Pawn Variation of the Winawer French Defense used to be. Without the activation of that specific part of my brain, I felt weak and watery.

Everything non-chess-related seemed silly. At parties, I watched the faces of my acquaintances flap away, dispensing sloppy trivialities that couldn't match the majesty of an unexpected move. "Shut the fuck up," I thought, ruefully. What good were the things I previously enjoyed? Once I had inhabited the realm of chess, full of violence and aesthetic beauty, but also replete with the restfulness of unambiguous actuality, my previous life was unappealing. When you quit chess, or try to, you don't just leave a game behind. You leave a world behind. It's painful. All I did was get drunk and circulate, inhabiting vague mental states in barrooms and living rooms.

And on one of these nights, I came home a little more drunk than usual and fired up a little blitz game. The next morning, having realized that I'd played chess the night before, I told myself that a slip isn't the same as a relapse, and I solemnly renewed my vow to never again move a single pawn. Six hours later, I had a full relapse—a week disappeared into a long session of unsatisfying blitz. Following this, I tried again, this time installing software that prevented me from accessing chess websites. A few days later, I came home drunk again and uninstalled the software. Another clump of days evaporated. Finally, it got so bad that I told myself I'd trade one addiction for another—I'd take up smoking again, which I had quit during my last month in Bangkok, in exchange for not playing chess. This is how I became a chain-smoking chess player.

There was only one disruption that got in the way of the complete domination, by chess, of my entire mental life. I was falling in love—with a person this time, and not a board game.

5

NO MACS

People love using chess as a metaphor. Supposedly, Brazilian jiu-jitsu is the most chess-like of the martial arts. One chef I knew, upon hearing of my passion for the game, characterized his selection of flavors as "a chess game I play with your mouth, bro." In the movie *Charlie Wilson's War,* a CIA weapons specialist is seen playing a simul in a park while simultaneously delivering a monologue about the artillery required to invade Afghanistan, a filmic juxtaposition which implies that military planning and middle-game strategy are complementary skills.

Part of me hates this tendency. After all, as I've mentioned, part of what makes chess wonderful is how much it *isn't* like all of this other shit we put up with on earth. On the other hand, I've made a few sweeping comparisons between life and chess already in this book, and it felt, as I was writing those passages, like I couldn't avoid doing so. Chess has a way of encircling the imagination, of generating fanciful poetics and dubious conceptual linkage. And I'm about to engage in another spell of that behavior right now.

It's true of both chess and life that sometimes an unwise move is unexpectedly fortuitous—sometimes a seeming mistake, or a moment of hotheaded flailing, provokes a situation that couldn't have been devised by sober strategy. For example, if I hadn't quite so terribly screwed up one of the writing assignments that I'd hurriedly completed while I prepared for the tournament in Bangkok, I never would have met Katherine.

She was a senior editor at a publication that demanded scrupulously written arts criticism based on diligent research. She had accepted one of my pitches, which promised that I'd write a thoughtful profile of one of my favorite Toronto painters. But instead, what I delivered to her inbox was a scrambled piece of mumbo jumbo, larded up with a few pretty sentences so she maybe wouldn't notice how bad it was. She noticed. After chopping up my piece to the extent that it miraculously became publishable, she sent me a stern email telling me that my work was unacceptable. I assumed she'd never want to speak to or work with me again. That assumption was incorrect. Somehow, she still thought I could contribute something worthwhile to the magazine. So, right around the time my chess addiction was coming back, she suggested we have coffee in order to improve our relationship.

We significantly improved our relationship. The air hurriedly rearranged itself when she entered the room. I knew immediately that I was in trouble. She was shockingly pretty, with glinting and mobile eyes, a chaotic cascade of blond hair, and a cherubic face that was frequently the home of a broad, wild smile. But her appearance wasn't what really got me. It was a certain kind of awareness. She was blessed and cursed with an unstoppable power of observation. While I drifted through life in a state of interior absorption, aware of little except my interior monologue, she missed nearly nothing, and her intelligence made something of every stimulus it encountered. It was a reactivity I could sense when I was around her—it was obvious that she was closer to the pulse of reality than I was. Being around that energy made me feel more alive than I usually was. After our initial meeting, I concluded that spending time without Katherine was objectively nonsensical.

We met for a subsequent coffee on a rainy day, during which meeting I did the obvious thing. I suggested that we do drugs together—specifically psilocybin, aka magic mushrooms. She agreed. After some discussion, we met where she was living, on Toronto Island, a clump of grass, sand, and charming houses in Lake Ontario. In her attic apartment, we scarfed down a few mushrooms coated with peanut butter, and, out in the sun, we found a little patch of beach overlooking the glassy condos that line the Toronto waterfront.

We lay down on the warm sand, and as the psilocybin kicked in, the day's green and blue grew bolder, becoming a ridiculous shade of lime and an implausible, unearthly ultramarine. Across the water, the buildings danced and broke apart, reassembling as they saw fit, often congealing in the shapes of punctuation marks drawn from alien alphabets. Katherine, after a long fit of giggling, was invited to a conference with a vein of horrid regrets that had been polished by her subconscious for this particular occasion. She started crying, so I brought her close to me. Her hand found mine in the dirt. Behind us, below a setting sun that was also the mouth of a mountain in the sky, a bunch of teens drank beer and laughed at us. They were comically long of limb, and their sinister faces were staticky and indistinct. Katherine suggested we hide from their judgment in her attic bedroom.

The walk took years, because the street before us kept growing longer as we pursued its end, and the houses on either side each had long and important messages to give us, which left deep grooves on the wax of our personalities. Resultantly, we were much older and much changed when we came up to her bedroom, and we sat in the purple dusk, amazed. We made it to her bed, where we lay side by side sobering up, listening to Drake, watching scattering motes of dust becoming tiny plumes of flame under the influence of the last of the light.

"I keep wondering whether we're gonna make out," I said. So we did.

With that, the rest of my life was all worked out. Katherine and I would be in love, because love is nice. We would remain together through the dimming of our initial lust. We would keep each other chuckling through our disappointments, and appreciate each other's little achievements. We would kiss some morning in Buenos Aires, and, on some other evening, lend each other warmth in a sketchy hotel room in Mongolia. Nothing stood in the way of our happiness.

Except, that is, for chess. That was the only exception. It was a big exception. My life was dominated by two forces that summer, like two magnetic poles, whose sway instilled in me a wobbly course. Some days, I was completely taken over by love and utterly involved in the banishment of my solitude. On other days, I fled inside myself and communed with the French Defense. But most of the time it was somewhere in between—I'd lose focus during a long game and think of the elegant slope of Katherine's stomach, or drift away, during a conversation with Katherine, to the mental composition of a middle-game strategy. This annoyed her, because it was annoying, and it annoyed me, too.

She tried to close this gap between us by picking up chess herself. But it didn't work out, because she didn't like how my personality changed when I sat down at the board. My usual persona during our relationship—goofy, supportive, affectionate—dropped away, replaced by a narrow seriousness. She hated it, so we played only a few times.

This was another great argument for quitting chess—that it was damaging to my new relationship, whether it took the form of a private emotional affair or a shared activity that Katherine didn't enjoy. I wanted to get with the plan, be a good boyfriend, and make some money so that we could get a cute house and a useless, stupid dog together. That kind of lifestyle was incompatible with playing eight hours a day. But I wasn't entirely persuaded by my best intentions.

I lived two lives: a public, romantic one with Katherine, and a private, shameful one with chess. Summer went by in a flash. Fall, which is clearly the reason for the rest of the year, said hello and then left abruptly. And the whole time, I was quitting chess about every other week. It was a big chunk of my year—dealing with the stresses of entertaining two different kinds of love. Everything else, as always, I did halfway.

As winter became a real threat, I started to realize that my rebellion was in vain—while I'd quit smoking once again, my chess addiction was brutally immovable. Chess was simply in me. Evidently, I couldn't do anything about that at the present moment. I wasn't done with it yet. Thus, the only question was what I was going to do about the overall state of affairs—what form of addicted life I would end up pursuing. Up until that point, with the exception of my one tournament game in Bangkok, my chess life mostly consisted of playing thousands of games at my computer, huddled and nonplussed. This was not satisfactory. It was lonely and unglamorous and possessed no drama beyond the momentary rages of one game or another. When I told my children about my twenties, I didn't want to explain that I spent big chunks of it in my bedroom staring at digital chess pieces, surrounded by granola bar wrappers, occasionally noticing the snow drifting by the window. And more importantly, I didn't want Katherine to see me abasing myself in such a fashion.

No. If I was going to be a victim of chess, like Duchamp, I was going to be a proud victim, like Duchamp. If I was going to waste my hours, I was at least going to waste them flamboyantly. Rather than skulking alone in my room, I decided, I would hold my head high. I would play in real tournaments, in countries near and far, for real money, against live, breathing opponents, hopefully with Katherine at my side, if she had nothing better to do and decided not to break up with me—if she didn't turn into my Lydie Sarazin-Levassor. Maybe I'd lose most of my games. Maybe I'd lose every game. But that would be okay, if not preferable. If I was to be remembered as a simpering incompetent, dismembered with comically simple tactics, so be it. Better that than be a vanishing piece of data on a server in an air-conditioned data center.

Furthermore, though I had been thinking of chess as

a diversion from being a human being, I realized that this wasn't altogether correct. After all, what do you think makes us human, exactly? What differentiates us from all the other carbon-based organisms merrily reproducing all over each other as much as possible? What makes us better and more interesting than a cloud of glowing fish?

One answer is: language. We're better because we talk so pretty. And because I make a living off language, it's tempting to agree. But, of course, the conversations of animals are pretty cool. Whales melodiously scream each other's names across the ocean currents. Mockingbirds, when they get tired of singing their own attractive songs, master the sayings of nearby toads. Fireflies' bodies are the canvases on which their messages flash. Although animal language might not possess the combinatorial depth of human language, it's still pretty faceted. So this isn't so clear.

Another answer is: tools—all of our intricate machines. Cordless drills are great. Any day I make a hole in something with a cordless drill is a good day. But tool use is found throughout the animal kingdom—the tools are less sophisticated, but they are tools. Crows sometimes make food-retrieving hooks out of discarded wire. Bottlenose dolphins stir up the sea floor in search of lunch with marine sponges held in their beaks. Chimpanzees, alarmingly, occasionally fashion spears for spearing galagos out of their galago-holes. Again, humans aren't alone in this category.

Our fashions are pretty cool—our cute little outfits—

but decorator crabs craft intricate camouflage out of stray materials with an arresting sense of natural style. Skyscrapers have always stirred a certain wonder in me, but I'm also intrigued by the carefully woven huts made by bowerbirds, or the lumpy castles built by termites.

And so on. Most human activities aren't uniquely human. They're different in degree of realization, because we've got opposable thumbs and a particularly sparkly topsoil of brain, but not different in fundamental kind.

In light of all this, in my opinion, if there's one particular thing that distinguishes us, it has to be abstraction. The way we take our fleshy, silt-covered world and cover it with metaphors, maps, formulas, and poems—how we incessantly make wickedly complicated models of everything we live in. According to us, the sea is wine-dark, the earth is composed of metropolitan areas, and some numbers are irrational.

If you accept this, I submit that chess is about the most human thing you can do. Lots of animals fight. But we say, okay, just as an experiment, instead of fighting with our actual bodies, maybe we could spar with teams of funny little wooden dolls, each of which moves in a different fashion, in a simulation of the stratification of human society. Then perhaps we'll come up with a whole language describing our imaginary battles, such that we might say, "Sasha played a subtle knight maneuver in the Czech Benoni." Eventually, someday, it's even possible that we'll develop computer programs that play this game better than we do.

Chess takes the most banal act of all—violence—and makes it a symbolic ballet with a culture entirely of its own. If there's anything that makes us better than butterflies, it's this kind of thing. We make cathedrals of pure thought from the bloody, nitty-gritty matters of simian life.

So then, rather than think of chess as a diversion from more important matters—politics, money, love—I could think of it, instead, as time spent worshipping the most remarkable properties of our species.

If you're not entirely convinced by this, I'm not either. Maybe semi-convinced. But it was something I could tell myself during the less glamorous moments of my journey.

Also, I girded myself with the knowledge that my first tournament game, in Bangkok, was definitely the worst game that I'd ever play. Although sickening defeats might yet follow, none would be as bad as my first devastating loss, which was more of a mental health episode than a competitive activity.

You should never do this. Never tell yourself you've been through the worst of anything.

■ ■ ■

I decided to set myself an ambitious goal that I would almost certainly fail to achieve, the key word being *almost*. I'd strive for the very edge of possibility. I couldn't become grandmaster, or a master at all. Becoming a surgeon was more likely. Becoming a frog was probably more likely. But I thought I could maybe, maybe, achieve a level of skill sufficient enough that I wouldn't immediately crumple, when playing the sport I love most, against any significant opposition. Enough that my brother, if we ever sat down for a serious game again, would have to watch his ass. Enough so that maybe I wouldn't completely hate myself.

Yes, I thought: in roughly a year, I would play in the Los Angeles Open, and I would beat a player whose rating was at least 2000. That would represent a violent assault against the limits of my truly meagre talent.

Why a 2000-rated player? Well, it's just such a satisfying number: those three zeroes standing neatly in a line. Also, the prospect brought me a sort of vicious glee, because I imagined that whoever had taken their rating past that second thousand would be quite proud of themselves. Proud enough that they'd feel extra bad when their position came crashing down before me.

For a first step, making it through a tournament game without crying or shitting my pants seemed like a good idea. This, I decided, was a simple matter of dulling my nervous system with experience. My knuckles needed quite a bit of bloodying before I frolicked with my fate in wonderful, dehydrated California. For the first few months, I resolved to play in any tournament I could get to, whether it was in Cairo, London, or under a nearby banana crate.

The world is lousy with chess tournaments. Almost

everywhere on earth, you can get checkmated and lose rating points. Mostly this is because setting up a tournament is really easy. Blinking requires only slightly more qualification. All you need is a chess federation—a bureaucracy that keeps track of who's great or terrible at chess—and an "arbiter," a rule-enforcing person certified by that organization who watches over the proceedings. Most of the rules are along the lines of "Don't talk" and "Don't touch your opponent" and "Don't make illegal moves."

Although the aforementioned FIDE is the major international bureaucracy, there are smaller bodies as well—many, many countries have federations of their own: Andorra, Ecuador, Tanzania, and even Canada, if you can believe that. Exploring the subject of chess governance more thoroughly is a tedious affair, so I won't do it. All you need to know is that FIDE-rated tournaments can take place in any country, but that rated tournaments aren't necessarily FIDE-rated tournaments. Playing in an Andorra tournament might just get you Andorra points, for example—each federation has a rating system of its own.

Not all tournaments are created equal. Most are inglorious little affairs conducted in church basements on weekends. You do battle with a crowd of local yokels at some pit stop in Michigan for a first-place prize of maybe five hundred dollars. Competitions like this don't attract elite players because they're not worth their time. They're busy playing closed invitational tournaments, like the prestigious

Bilbao Masters, for a chance at 150,000 euros, or occasionally destroying all comers at open tournaments, like the Reykjavik Open, for a mere five grand or so. Economically, chess is sort of like acting: top people make money, second-rate people teach, and everyone else receives spotty compensation at best.

The two types of tournaments have completely different emotional valences. Low-level tournaments are resplendent with spiritual hunger. Nobody is so concerned with their place in the pecking order as the middling player—the middle-aged accountant who's out to prove that he's the best of his city's almost-masters. Adding to the fervor is the fact that young players are sometimes in competition for a chess scholarship from an American school, meaning that a good showing against the regional competition might be one step towards a full ride at the University of Texas.

Meanwhile, top-tier tournaments are calm, buttoned-down affairs, sponsored by energy companies and banks, taking place in spacious, teal-carpeted venues. The players are eminently comfortable professionals who are treated as such: they're flown in and put up in four-star hotels. Although they're looking to play their best, they're mostly not that worried, partially because, at the top level of the invitational circuit, even a fifth-place showing is financially rewarded. Assured, charcoal-blazered, and regal in their bearing, the stars of the game are followed across lobbies by the chess press gang, a strange micro-community that watches their movements closely, whether in London, Qatar, or Baku. Closing ceremonies typically feature jazz combos and plastic cups of cheap prosecco. In terms of atmosphere, these events are halfway between Wimbledon and a spelling bee.

My first tournament in Canada was one of the local yokel–type affairs, taking place a short walk from my apartment, a few weeks after my decision to play real chess like a real person. The night of my first game, big, thick snowflakes were falling all around, coating everything. It was one of those winter nights when the density of weather obliterates all the specifics of your surroundings, when you might as well be walking through any other storm in any other year.

Katherine came along. While she didn't really care about watching the games themselves, she liked that I was regarding chess as a legitimate love rather than a shameful and private disease. It was a change in attitude that made me a bit less of an asshole. Previously, the more I resisted chess, the more it seized my consciousness. It grabbed the end of every train of thought, pulling each partial sentiment downwards to the corner of my mind where the chessboard resided. But when I finally gave in, and earnestly decided to study, improve, and checkmate an intercontinental fleet of nitwits, I found myself more able to enjoy other parts of life, knowing that after a dinner out with Katherine at our favorite restaurant, I wouldn't have to apologize for wanting to look up the score of the latest Ivanchuk game when we got back to my apartment.

Out of the snow, we arrived at a meeting of the Annex Chess Club in Toronto. It was a group of charming, mostly sedate people playing blitz games in a community center. After paying my registration fee, I sat in the corner, wondering who would soon destroy me. Would it be the mop-topped kid with the cool military jacket? Or the old woman with pearl earrings? Katherine brought me coffee, played with my hair, and told me I'd be fine.

There's a menacing lull that precedes all open chess tournaments—a silence tinted by the excitement of incipient conflict felt by a roomful of dorks awaiting their fate. That fate is determined, during those long moments, by the arbiters, who run an algorithm that determines the pairings. Then, when the arbiters print the pairings and tape them to the far wall, the players follow and form a clump, all briefly squinting together at the future they've been assigned before scattering to meet it. Also, the computers are always beat-up old PCs. There are no Macs in the chess world. The anthropological significance of this is left to the reader.

GAME 2 SASHA CHAPIN VS. LASAGNA DAVIES

I sat down at board 45. (The boards at a tournament are ranked based on tournament standing, with the leaders playing at board 1.) My opponent was a little late. Since I couldn't contain myself, I asked a friendly man at the next board whether I should be scared of him.

"He's a really nervous guy," he said, "so just play calmly and you'll be fine."

"Calm is one thing I absolutely cannot do," I said.

"Just be calmer than he is."

"Do you think I can do that?"

"It would be hard not to."

"So just play solid until he falls apart."

"Exactly."

As soon as that last word was uttered, Lasagna showed up. He was a short man of maybe thirty whose face was fixed in an expression of gleeful fear.

"You are probably strong player," he said.

"I'm actually unrated in Canada," I said.

"So you are one of these Internet guys."

"I, well, yeah, I play on the Internet."

"Learning all your Internet things, now you come kill me."

"That, uh, may be accurate."

"I see this in your eyes. This will be very difficult."

"For one of us, I'm not sure who."

He buried his head in his hands.

"Oh no," he said. "No."

For a chess player, Lasagna didn't like chess very much. Every move seemingly caused him physical pain. His hands shook as he reached for each piece, and when he hurriedly deposited each one on its chosen square, he winced and clenched his fists. "Oh no," he murmured again, after I'd made a completely routine move. He stared at the board, dumbfounded by a fairly sedate position. It was a Queen's Gambit Declined, the same sort of solid, boring setup I'd had in my game with Diaphragm.

But in this game I wasn't so self-destructive. The first fifteen moves were pretty normal. We engaged in quiet maneuvers, gently jostling for space on the board, sizing each other up. But it was a quietude that didn't last long. Most games between lower-rated players end when someone misses a simple trick. While higher-rated players are like seismographs, capable of responding precisely to the most distant tremors, lower-rated players are like drunkards playing with dynamite, as liable to blow themselves up as to accomplish anything else.

In this case, Lasagna missed what chess players call a "pin," a situation in which your piece can't do anything because it's shielding a vital piece standing behind it. After a series of moves I tricked him into, one of his most important pawns couldn't move, because it had to remain in place and protect his queen. This meant it was unable to defend a pawn next to it, the capture of which would immediately destroy his position.

Fifteen minutes passed while I stared at the obvious winning move, because I didn't quite believe that an obvious winning move could occur in a game I played. Eventually, I took the pawn, after checking and rechecking my calculations.

"What is this?" he said.

(Lasagna always talked during his games, an illegal habit that continued no matter how often he was chastised by the arbiters, who, in lily-livered Canadian fashion, never actually ejected him.)

"Just a simple tactic," I said.

After squinting at the pieces for a moment, he realized what had occurred.

"Why do they play such moves against me?" he asked, to which I offered no reply.

It was all over after that. The game wasn't technically lost—a computer, given his position, probably could've figured out a draw—but he was facing an uphill battle in a state of unabating misery. Every subsequent breath he took at the board was pulled through clenched teeth. He played like a hooked fish for the rest of the game, then resigned.

"You are strong player," he said, afterwards.

"I just got lucky," I said.

"Good player is always lucky."

"Bad players are occasionally lucky also."

After further objections, he began ranting nonspecifically about rating points, before being interrupted by Katherine embracing me.

"Good job, baby," she said.

"I can actually win games sometimes."

"Yeah, you can."

"It feels so weird."

Lasagna followed us out into the adjoining hall, still speaking loudly about all of the wonderful numbers I would receive. We politely said words and then left. Outside, the snowstorm was over. My face was freezing, but I couldn't feel anything but a pure, childlike enthusiasm. I wouldn't have believed you if you told me I wasn't the mayor of all existence. Diamonds filled the air, I was sure, which I could pluck out at any time. Every ten feet I interrupted Katherine with a sloppy kiss.

And this already wild happiness was only multiplied when I won the next round, in a similar fashion, a week later. Not only had I won my first two Canadian tournament games, I'd actually won the whole tournament—or at least its beginner section, for players rated under 1800—because it was canceled after two rounds, for arcane scheduling reasons I didn't care about.

Chess! Not that hard, as it turns out. Not for a guy like me.

6

ROUGH GUS

I woke suffused with excitement on the day of the next tournament on my Toronto schedule, the Hart House Open. As I prepared my morning coffee, I jangled around the kitchen delightedly, knowing I'd deliver a stunning performance that would scintillate the chess community, and maybe impress Katherine, slightly. I'd finally feel unambiguously good about myself—capable of love, capable of chess, a human being deserving of his allotted portion of white blood cells. The kids who bullied me when I was younger would hear about my tour de force, and they'd feel bad, as they should.

The tournament was named for the building it was held in, Hart House, an old faux-medieval building belonging to the University of Toronto, where zany activities happen. The morning of the tournament was clear, cool, and bright. I smiled at the world genteelly, with Katherine on my arm, as I entered the tournament hall, which was a gigantic dining room whose wood walls bore clusters of engraved Latin mottos. My Latin is rusty, so I was free to imagine that the mottos were all predictions of the wanton wrath I'd inflict upon the children before me.

There were a lot of children. Basically, my bracket of the Hart House Open was me, thirty Chinese kids, and a couple of other Caucasian-ish people of various ages. Essentially, I was attending a Chinese kid convention. This made me feel more than a little out of place. It slightly disturbed my pluckiness. I couldn't help but recall my wasted youth, which had far too little chess in it, and far too many soggy sandwiches, occasionally seasoned by stray tears. Meanwhile, here were a hundred jubilant kids, many with charming bowl cuts, whose parents were always close at hand, helping them achieve chess greatness. They stared at me, parents and children, seemingly wondering why I'd been pulled from a sarcophagus and placed in their playground. It was a weird dynamic.

But, "Fuck it," I thought. Somebody had to teach them that life wasn't going to be all roses and hamburgers. They should be disabused of the notion that the world would immediately yield to their desires upon seeing their squishy young faces. I would deliver that news, borne on the thrusts of my bishops.

This is one of the embarrassing things about coming to chess in your twenties. When you're in the lower ranks, your opponents are basically of two varieties: children with promise who haven't yet developed their skills, and adults who are long past their peak, too old to calculate complicated tactics. Meanwhile, you float in the middle, in a state of static mediocrity.

Katherine got me coffee, then mimicked the facial expression of an interested person as my first game began.

GAME 4 SASHA CHAPIN VS. HARRY HUNCHES

My approach to this game was highly original. You might say it was bold and unpredictable. I played with an artistic and mercurial style. After making ten perfect moves, which made my opponent sulk like his mom just took away his Internet privileges, I started playing like an energetic moron. Diligently, I equalized a game in which I'd enjoyed a tremendous advantage, then mounted an attack that didn't really attack anything. Following my completely silly offensive, my pieces were all over the place, making their capture quite literally child's play. During this last stage of the game, Harry's friends all sat next to the board, smiling and fidgeting.

"Good game," I said, shaking Harry's hand. Wordlessly, shyly, he returned my handshake, then left.

"Aw man, I'm sorry," Katherine said.

"I can never play that badly again," I said.

"Wanna go get a burrito?"

"I don't know."

"You'll feel better after a burrito."

"I feel nothing but rage, and I am its only object."

"Don't be so hard on yourself."

"But the correct assessment of the situation is that I'm a fucking idiot who should never do anything again."

"Look, the first ten moves were good, right?"

"Yeah, until I self-destructed, I was playing high-quality chess."

"So that shows you that you've just got to pay attention and not let go."

"What you're saying isn't literally impossible."

"Dude, you're gonna do great."

"Jesus, I fucking hope so."

After our burrito, Katherine had work to do, so I went back alone, armed with her wonderful, cleansing love and my useless mind. Full of molten self-revulsion and beans, I sat alone in a lounge abutting the playing hall—it was an hour until the next round, and the kids were frolicking all around me, having a great time. Among them was little Harry Hunches, zapping his friends with an imaginary ray gun, *zap zap.*

My mind grew blacker with every breath I took, so I tried to breathe infrequently. Momentarily, the pairings for the next round were posted. With as neutral a facial expression as possible, I greeted my opponent, Rough Gus.

GAME 5 ROUGH GUS VS. SASHA CHAPIN

The thing about being beaten by a little kid is, like, I'm better than a little kid, right? Any impartial observer would have to agree that I am superior to nearly any ten-year-old. While I'm maybe not as cherubic or delicate, I am more tough, useful, steadfast, reasonable, caring, intelligent, precise, and voluminous. Most children can't lift three hundred pounds, as I can. Painful years have abraded the superfluities of my personality. Come over sometime and I'll cook a fantastic meal as long as you bring the wine I suggest. Only an idiot or a pervert would want to hang out with Rough Gus, my opponent, instead of me.

And yet, Rough Gus bested me. Admittedly, I helped him out quite a bit by playing terribly. Concentration, the most important mental resource in chess, was something I simply couldn't summon at that moment—only rage—rage at the previous game, and rage at Rough Gus's behavior.

Rough Gus was a weird, weird kid. For most of the game he stared at a bottle of iced tea, which he swirled around until it frothed. Occasionally he took breaks from that, during which he tore strips out of the bottle's label and tied them in delicate knots. Twice, he got up, went over to the wall, and rubbed a small patch of it for thirty seconds or so. He never looked at me. And never did he betray any sign that he regarded our game as more important than any of his other fidgety little activities.

Defeat was swift and terrible.

Outside, a superlative sunset could be seen quivering in melted snow puddles all down the quiet street. Among this excellent weather I felt ghastly. Along the way home I ran into an old friend who had recently dealt with cancer. He was happy. Seeing that I was not, he provided encouraging words.

There is little point in discussing the next few games in detail. The grotesquerie continued. I lost my next game, against a young man who was terribly affected by eczema—some of his facial skin fell on my pieces as he took them from me one by one. I then lost another. During the last game, I was barely conscious, so I hardly noticed when I lost that one, too. My opponent was a mean old man. The kind I would become if my life continued like this.

That was it. The tournament was over. The flocks of children scattered homewards—full of joy, full of potential. Where I went, there was only white-hot agitation. I was a hive of putrid thoughts, each ultimately becoming an argument proving my own inadequacy, finding evidence from every corner of my memory. Everyone had seen this coming, the failure I now was. My grade school teachers—they all knew what was going on. There goes little Sasha. What will become of that unkempt boy? I don't know, but thinking about it makes me sad.

I left my apartment after screaming incoherently in the shower and went over to Katherine's and slept badly. When I woke at noon, she was stroking my hair.

"Good morning, li'l pal, how are you feeling?" she said.

"I've never been so happy," I said.

"Oh yeah?"

"I'm completely ecstatic."

"It's really not so bad—you'll play better next time."

"But will I?"

"You couldn't play much worse."

"Honestly I don't understand it—I thought I was getting better."

"Maybe you just had a bad tournament."

"Maybe."

But I couldn't accept that rationale. There had to be a reason why I'd played so badly, after playing so well. I couldn't blame the mere fact of human frailty. Doing that would be giving up. I would be forsaking all hope of improvement, and surrendering to the possibility that I'd forever oscillate between being middling and pitiable.

What followed was a few solid months of trying to improve myself with self-authored techniques. My efforts were an unremitting deluge of inanity. The problem with trying to solve your own psychological problems is that you're inside the delusion you're trying to diagnose. Being a bad chess player, I came up with a series of bad solutions to my bad chess play. I wallowed in a mess of my own dubious pseudo-insights, developing a whole rotisserie of far-fetched and spurious strategies.

For example: at one point, I hit upon the idea that maybe

the essential ingredient to good chess play was self-hatred. After all, I'd played well at the Annex Chess Club tournament, which I'd begun in a state of shameful terror, but I played badly at Hart House after entering the competition in good spirits. Therefore, I should try to feel unhappy before every match. This was bulletproof reasoning, I thought.

So, when I played a small weekend tournament in Ottawa a few weeks after Hart House, I made sure to be as sad and uncomfortable as possible. I wrote "you have no talent" on my palm, drank jugs of ice water until I shivered, and sat on my hands for the whole of every game. And I won my bracket. "Problem solved," I thought. "Just feel bad, and you'll checkmate everybody." But then I applied the same strategy to a subsequent tournament in Manhattan, and I lost every game.

Clearly, I needed to stop relying on my own judgment. What I really needed was a teacher—someone who could actually figure out why I was so terrible. One name came to mind instantly: that of Grandmaster Ben Finegold.

7

THE SECRET OF CHESS

first stumbled upon the lectures of my future teacher and spiritual guardian, Ben Finegold, during a despairing google for chess tips in Bangkok. He was different from all the other chess lecturers I'd seen before. Most lecturing grandmasters, even the most charming ones, approach the game with a hushed reverence, as if delivering news on a pediatric oncology ward, or trying to placate an errant tiger. Finegold is the complete opposite. He's charismatic, frank, and viciously funny, matching a respect for the game's elegance with flagrant mockery of everything else. When Finegold's students raise their hands, he often points a meaty hand at them and says, "You, with the wrong answer," or "You, with some crazy comment." Upon hearing one of their replies, he'll often respond, "Ugh, that was painful," or "Hey, you're the best player in your chair." He's given to claiming that the Panov-Botvinnik Attack was named after

"Mr. Attack." His lectures are littered with Tarantino references, imitations of other lecturers from his chess club, and fatuous advice like "never move pawns."

I soon felt like he was someone I'd already known my entire life. He reminded me of my stereotypically Jewish relatives, who communicated their affection with scabrousness and sarcasm, just like they communicated everything else. I found his lectures so comforting that I often left them playing in my apartment on my laptop during cigarette breaks or other interregna—his voice came wafting out to the balcony and took on a strange gravity under the starlight.

He isn't always the most informative lecturer. His lectures are as much about verbiage as they are about chess. Sometimes, if a game he's showing a class bores him, he'll say things like, "Enh, this seems like a chess position," or "We need some smelling salts for the audience." But he communicates a powerful if occasionally clumsy affinity for the game that I enjoy much more than the highfalutin academicism displayed by other teachers.

Finegold has a unique place in the chess world. He has ardent fans, because of his aforementioned characteristics, and many detractors, also because of his aforementioned characteristics. Moreover, he lives on an odd plateau of chess skill—that of the low-level grandmaster. The fact that this is a coherent concept is another illustration of the vast distance between the amateur and the professional player. To any player like me, any grandmaster lives in an unreachable and starry grove of intellectual superiority. Someone like Finegold can calculate in drunken sleep better than I can while achieving satori on Adderall. But, to most grandmasters, Finegold isn't that notable, except for his personality. Like in any professional sport, the best of the best chess players have to live with being forever inferior to the best of the best of the best. While Finegold occasionally scores an upset, like a win against Shakhriyar Mamedyarov, a player consistently in the world's top ten, he mostly can't compete with the top-flight professionals.

There are essentially two ways you could regard Finegold, given his position in the chess ecosystem. You could see him as a pitiable example of the game's mercilessness, by focusing on the fact that Finegold never made it to the upper ranks. On the other hand, you could see him as someone who hurled himself directly into the howling void of chess and came out intact, with a fan following, two kids, a little house in Georgia, and the ability to eke out a modest living by teaching his favorite game to captivated pupils—occasionally including desperate adults who come all the way from Canada to absorb his teachings.

After I'd won the tournament in Ottawa, but also faced disaster in Manhattan, when I felt desperate and lost and in need of guidance, I shot him an email, to see if he'd give me some private lessons. He agreed, and told me to meet him a couple of months later in St. Louis, where he had a teaching residency over the summer.

Katherine's reaction to the news that I was planning to spend a month in St. Louis was decidedly mixed. She knew how important Finegold was to me. And in a way, he was important to her, too, because a lot of my mannerisms that she found most charming were actually Finegoldisms that had crept their way into my vocabulary. He was, she knew, like a second father I'd never met, and she was delighted that I'd have the chance to finally sit across from him. Maybe he would even rouse me from the half-stupor I'd been in ever since Hart House. On the other hand, like, what the fuck, right? Her boyfriend was going to leave her for a month, during the pleasant first year of the relationship, to spend time in a hot, dangerous American city for, yet again, the sake of a nerdy, juvenile hobby.

These contradictions went unresolved throughout the two months following my first communication with Finegold, during which I attempted to prepare for his tutelage with more mostly fruitless practice. It was a time of tension, after which Katherine drove me to the airport and kissed me goodbye, in a state composed of several sentiments hanging together like the molecules in margarine.

■ ■ ■

I arrived in St. Louis a few days before my first meeting with Finegold, to have a chance to explore the city. And during this pre-Finegold interval, I had a random meeting with a stranger that would prove to be an omen of the month ahead. She was a woman walking alone downtown, screaming.

"Are you okay?" I asked.

"Holy shit," she screamed.

"Um," I said.

"Fuck all of these pussy-ass people," she screamed.

"This city is hell on earth," she screamed.

"I am so tired of this life," she screamed.

"Damn it," she screamed.

"The sun is too hot," she screamed.

She walked away. And, unfortunately, I came to agree with her about the city of St. Louis.

This is probably my fault. I am a great believer in the idea that a failure to love is often the fault of the lover. If I were more patient and more curious and more forgiving, I probably could've found more to appreciate. I'm told that St. Louis contains many beautiful sun-strewn lanes, and cheerful people, and fun bars where tender words are exchanged over locally made beers of the highest quality. But that is not what I found. What I found was a humid, boring, and flat place, dappled with some of the most dangerous neighborhoods in North America. According to the website of the St. Louis Police, you shouldn't "wear clothing or shoes that restrict your movement" in their fair metropolis, so you can run away from assailants if you need to.

The local food, also, is hilarious. There's a special kind of pizza they make there, which is a prank played by Satan. It's a cracker, topped with ketchup, finished with a goopy kind of processed cheese that you've never had before, because they invented a new kind of cheese for this pizza. It's edible caulking that clings to the back of your throat, reminding you that you live in an unjust world.

Based on my experiences, I cannot recommend St. Louis. Unless, that is, you're interested in studying chess. Weirdly, St. Louis is the home of the world's best chess school. This unexpected juxtaposition exists because of the fact that chess is the greatest love of billionaire Rex Sinquefield, a longtime St. Louis resident. Although he was never a skilled player, he was a skilled investor, to say the least, and he arrived at retirement age with enough money that he could quite casually open an air-conditioned temple devoted to his favorite game, and bankroll grandmaster lectures as well as exclusive tournaments with big prizes for the strongest players in the world. The club is housed in a pristine two-story commercial property, and might be mistaken for a posh hernia clinic or a yoga studio if not for the chess pieces depicted on the frontispiece's stained glass windows.

As with many chess clubs, the social scene is a mix of a few demographics who couldn't possibly understand one another in any other setting. There are the rich kids, clad in spotless primary colors, hair thick with drugstore pomade, murmuring conspiratorially about what they've learned in recent grandmaster lessons. There are old men in fanny packs lounging around them, wearing faded T-shirts, thumbing ancient chess paperbacks far from their original relevance. Middle-aged Slavs and Cypriots walk from room to room with the confidence of former World Champions, and are occasionally, in fact, former World Champions. Young staff in uniform red polos watch everything wearily and collaborate on difficult puzzles behind the front desk during the quieter hours of the day.

I showed up when I was told to, signed up for a membership, and hung around the lobby surveying the local milieu until Finegold entered a few minutes later. It was funny seeing him in life, after having watched his face move for so many hours. Ben is a combination of scary-looking and adorable. His hooded eyes and hooked nose give him a severity of expression that would serve the social purposes of a vicious mafioso or a disapproving rabbi. He's broad, squat, and heavy, and has an intense gaze that sometimes indicates that you've been singled out for special criticism among all of the creatures in existence. But his mouth is often settled in an amused smirk, he's always in a grumpy kind of good cheer, and his gravelly voice has a cryptic musicality that makes it sound like he's been telling one long joke for his entire life, a joke which may or may not eventually find a punchline.

"Hey, Finegold," I said.

"Sup," he said.

"I'm Sasha, that Canadian guy."

"Who?"

"That guy who emailed you."

"I know who you are."

"Yeah, so, here I am."

"How many lessons are you looking for?"

"I was thinking like ten hours."

"You could do more—the more you pay, the more you learn."

As I considered this, a class of kids, whom he had just taught, flooded out of the classroom and started playing blitz in the lobby, which is to say that they started knocking pieces off tables, knocking clocks off tables, making illegal moves, and screaming at each other. Finegold presided for a few minutes until the parents showed up, delighting the kids with a barrage of verbal abuse, and then returned to me with a searching look on his face.

"Jesus, I want to kill myself," he said, very quietly.

"Wait till you see my games," I said.

"You're not here to impress me, you're here to learn."

"But I'd like to impress you."

"Well, you won't."

And he was right. He was right about everything. Sooner or later, everything he told me came true.

Don't Lose All Your Pieces

During the first lesson, Finegold asked me to show him some of my games. And of course I wanted to wow him, even though he'd told me that was impossible. I wanted him to tell me that my sadness was misplaced, that I was secretly brilliant, that he could unearth my potential instantly, perhaps with an incantation of several magic words, accompanied by the wiggling of his fingers. To get that process going, I showed him one of my victories from Ottawa, in which I had the white pieces against a man named Loamy Washington. It was the game I was proudest of.

Being desperate for Finegold's approval, I elaborately soliloquized about the game as I played it out on a board between us, interrupting the narration to explain the stategical ideas behind every move, saving special drama for the last few moves preceding checkmate. It was like an unmetered poem, stuffed with misplaced enthusiasm. Finegold interrupted with minor criticism of some of my decisions, but mostly he just listened. And after my summary, he gathered his thoughts for a moment and I waited for him to express his admiration for what I'd presented.

"Okay," he said, "you just said a lot of fancy stuff, but I didn't really hear any of it. What I heard was that you played some decent moves, and your opponent played some decent moves, and then he lost his rook. Basically, we could've stopped after that. Okay, so maybe your technique could've been improved a little bit. But what happened is that he blundered. And you didn't blunder. Show me another game."

So I showed him one of the games from New York City

where I lost, terribly. Again, I spoke at great volume, detailing all of the intricacies of my frustrated plans.

"Okay, so, again," he said, "what happened here is that you fucked up, and you're just saying it in a fancy way. You had a nice position. You would've won from that position, eleven days out of ten, if you were a grandmaster. And then you lost all your pieces. That's it. And this is what I teach my students. You come in here, and you're like, show me how to play like Carlsen, show me this weird checkmate. And I look at your games, and all that happens is that you lose all your pieces, or you don't. When you're an advanced student, you can worry about more complicated stuff. But until then, I'll teach you how to avoid losing your pieces."

He cleared his throat.

"So anyway," he said, "what's your goal in chess?"

"I want to beat a 2000-rated player," I said.

"You'll probably do that, and the reason you will, is you won't blunder away your pieces."

"Really?"

"Yes—your problem isn't as complicated as you think it is."

Those were such reassuring words. And such terrible words. Because Finegold was implying that my defects were utterly common. He had seen students like me before. He would also see them again. And all of us were suffering from the same ailment. And it was absolutely mundane.

I don't know why this came as such a surprise. It's not like any of my other problems are terribly interesting. They're all pretty normal. Like "first love is annoyingly memorable." And "life is short and weird and full of danger." And "suffering always finds you, even in your beautifully decorated apartment."

Every year, I discover, more and more, that I'm the same as everyone else. Which is kind of great, because it means that life is not so mysterious. You just do what other people do. Say please. Floss. When you're making scrambled eggs, stir them really fast so they don't get crusty. Find a few good people and try to hang on to them. Don't lose all your pieces.

Just Because Someone Goes Crazy, It Doesn't Mean You Also Have to Go Crazy

"If your wife cheats on you, that's bad," Finegold said. "She shouldn't have done that. But if you then kill her, kill yourself, and the mailman, that's not really constructive. You shouldn't escalate a situation just because someone else did."

"How does this apply to chess?" I said.

"Well, you consider yourself a creative guy, which is kind of a problem. So, from move two, you're going out of your mind, trying to invent a work of genius. Which means that when your opponents play crazy, you start playing even crazier. Don't do that. Just don't be crazy at all. When they play weird, just play normal good moves. Other grandmasters will tell you that you have to punish your opponents for all of their mistakes. That's one point of view. My point of view is that you have to win chess games."

The wisdom of this became clear after the lesson, when we played some blitz at one of the tables set up on the sidewalk outside the club. The muggy air was licking my face. Cute couples walked by on their way to Whole Foods, unaware that they were passing a spectacle of truly historic importance: my first game against a grandmaster. It was also the first time I'd ever played against someone drinking two brands of seltzer at once. Finegold played the Slav Defense, an extremely solid opening.

"I hate playing against the Slav," I said.

"The truth hurts," he said.

"Is this a good move?"

"It's a move."

"But is it good?"

"Probably not. Whose turn is it?"

He moved his queen deep into my territory. For the first ten moves, I thought I might have a microscopic chance of victory, because I didn't lose all of my pieces. But, every other turn, I made a slight mistake that I didn't know I was making, and in the face of my craziness, he responded not with theatrics but with quiet malice. As sweat dripped down my chest, I realized that a crowd was gathering—all the kids in the neighborhood wanted to see Finegold crush me. I tried to put up a good fight so I could entertain these little boys and girls, who were soon to be embittered adults, maybe losing at chess themselves. But Finegold didn't give me a good fight—he gave me a slow, vicious grind, allowing me only to twist lamely while he attained total control. I was a jittery rabbit, running from a surefooted cheetah, in a maze whose pathways slowly curled in on each other and contracted, until we were confined together, predator and prey, in a tiny cell. Under the pressure, I cracked, and made a horrible blunder.

"You'll have to forgive him for that," Finegold said to the audience. "He's tired, because he just moved here. From Crazytown."

Never Resign

All night, screams came from outside my window. They were happy screams, at first, but soon they became angry screams. Apparently, the house party across the street was turning into a violent melee. The police arrived, and blessed silence returned, until maybe fifteen minutes later, when a spell of gunshots in the distance was rewarded by the sound of many others. My nerves were inconsolable, and I couldn't sleep.

And as the wet, waxy dawn crept across the window, I left the house and went down the street to the café where everyone hated me. Why they did, I'm not sure—I was always polite and I tipped generously. But their contempt was palpable. Every time I bought their coffee, I was given a cold, flat stare, which I returned. We were all clear on who liked each other. Nobody liked anybody. This happened every day. Then I took a bus and then a train to the club. You'll be happy to know that the St. Louis metro officially forbids weapons, and advertises this in every train car.

When I got to the club the day after the nighttime excitement, a few days after I had first enrolled, I met up with Isaac Schrantz, an employee whom I'd become chummy with on the basis of a shared intuition that we were equally unskilled. We'd established a series of officially rated games, which we called the Good Guys Fun Times Classic. This was possible because essentially everyone who worked there was a certified arbiter, so you could show up at any time of day and declare your intention to get checkmated in an official manner.

Due to my insomnia, I was a mess. This was not aided by another gigantic coffee from Starbucks I was drinking as I came in. Never before had my motion so resembled that of a despairing hummingbird. I was pale as a clammy baby and all the wrong kinds of sensuous. Finegold was hanging around the front desk as I came in.

"Hey, where's my Starbucks?" he said.

"I didn't know you would be here," I said.

"Well, now you know."

"I'll get you some coffee after I checkmate Isaac. Hey, Isaac."

"Sup," said Isaac.

We went upstairs and commenced our game. Finegold

didn't have to wait long for coffee, but it wasn't because I delivered checkmate. About ten moves in, because of my fidgetiness, I ran afoul of a merciless rule of tournament chess: the touch-move rule. You touch a piece, you've got to move it.

Erroneously, I tapped my bishop. Which immediately implied that I had to send it uselessly out onto a random square on the board, which, in turn, meant that Isaac got to take one of my knights for free. This was all so depressing that I immediately gave up. After we shook hands, and he consoled me, I went downstairs to the front desk and told Finegold, who was hanging out on the sofa and mocking his colleagues, that I could start my lesson early. His complexion deepened.

From our first lesson, Finegold was always telling me how mad he was. Everything I did angered him, apparently. "I've never been so furious," he'd say. Or "I'm sooo mad." But he didn't seem mad at all, really. His tone remained jolly, even as he was insulting my every decision. But when we sat down together, during this, our fourth consultation, he looked at me with genuine anger. It was a look that nearly made my testicles fall off.

"So," he said, "I assume you resigned."

"That's correct."

"You're not allowed to do that. You're my student. Why did you resign?"

"I lost a piece because I touched the wrong bishop."

"That's no excuse. You keep fighting."

"It was so depressing."

"I don't care. You have to put your whole being into chess. You can't just say, 'I'm tired, I'm sad, I don't want to play today.' That won't get you anywhere. You keep fighting. And you'll win. Because all the players you're playing are lousy players, by my standards. These idiots you're dealing with, they'll give you a chance. Seven days a week, I'd bet that Isaac, if you kept playing your heart out, would give you a piece back. Do you want to play like a top player? If Bobby Fischer had lost his bishop, he'd keep playing Isaac. And he'd win. My students are not allowed to resign."

It had been a long time since an adult had told me I wasn't allowed to do something. The feeling was reassuring.

"Are you playing in the rapid tournament tonight?" he said.

"Yes," I said.

"Don't resign. And try to get some sleep beforehand."

"Okay."

I did not get more sleep. When I returned to the club, Finegold confronted me.

"Did you sleep?" he said.

"No," I said.

"Ach," he said, and threw up his hands. I headed upstairs with the other players to be assigned to a section. It was a weekly tournament, where the stakes were a small cash prize and an even smaller boost to your local reputation. We were placed in groups of four based on our rating. My quad contained an old man who was fragrantly drunk, a cheery boy of twelve, and a muscular trash-talker with wraparound shades.

During my first game, against the kid, I immediately lost a piece. The urge to resign was almost overwhelming. But instead, I did what I learned to do with my bachelor's degree in literature: boldly assert a bunch of nonsense. In response, he lost all his pieces. After I won, I went downstairs.

"So how did you lose this time?" Finegold said.

"I actually won," I said.

"Shocking."

"I didn't resign, like you said."

"How did the game go?"

"Sort of a boring queen's pawn opening, and I immediately lost a piece, but then I started screwing with him, and tricked him into a winning endgame where I was up material."

"Sounds like the Picture of Dorian fuckin' Gray," he said, and left the room.

I won the rest of my games, and collected my prize money.

Have Less Fun

Afraid of the crime, about which I'd been cautioned by roughly every resident of St. Louis I'd talked to, I hung around outside the chess club for most of every day. It's situated in one of the safest pockets of the downtown. This doesn't mean that it's totally crime-free—a few weeks after I left, ten people were robbed at gunpoint by the metro station a couple of blocks away. But it's generally okay. The worst thing that happens, if you hang around the building all day, is you end up developing a habit of playing blitz with the local street chess players.

There's no precise definition of street chess. Most street chess happens outdoors, in parks around the world, but not all outdoor chess is street chess. It's sort of a matter of style and attitude. Street players generally play a beautiful kind of nonsense. If they can't play an aggressive move, they'll play an absurd move, so you're always on the run or trying to figure out what the fuck is going on. It's the kind of foofaraw that grandmasters find laughable but that can terrify and confuse intermediate players. And while this style doesn't work in serious long games, it's surprisingly effective in blitz, where verve matters as much as correctness.

They also hone their trash-talking skills as much as their chess. Sometimes these aptitudes can clinch the game, as in my game with Robert, one of the more competent members of the local brigade. I was crushing him, and then he started singing, "Why can't we be friends? Why can't we be friends?" in a surprisingly arresting tenor. He sang it over and over again, louder and less tunefully each time, making unbroken eye contact, until he was essentially shouting at me about my insufficient friendliness. Distracted, I lost all my pieces.

But this kind of warfare doesn't always work out. Another player, Art, told me that he was so named because of the artistic nature of his play, whose intricacies I would never grasp—he could tell, he said, at length, that I was a crude person who would never understand the philosophy that underpinned his moves. Dazzled by the logic of his own pontification, he didn't notice what I was up to. "Yeah, I guess I just don't get it," I said, as I delivered checkmate.

Finegold, who was always coming and going, and who noticed everything, observed that I was having a lot of fun, and that it was translating into my play as a whole. I was becoming sillier and more reckless, both in rated games I played around the club, and in casual games between the two of us. He disapproved.

"Take a look at those guys over there," he said, during a lesson, pointing to an array of portraits of great players that hung on the far wall.

"What am I supposed to be seeing?" I said.

"Tell me who looks like he's never had fun in his life."

"Um, Kasparov."

Garry Kasparov was the top-ranked player in the world for nineteen years, except for a three-month-long slump. And he was famous for his boundless, masochistic work ethic. "Chess is mental torture," he said. After he won a brilliant game, he'd take his scoresheet home and castigate himself for his inconsequential mistakes.

"Yeah, Kasparov never had any fun. Now, tell me who looks like he's furious all the time."

"Bobby Fischer."

It's occasionally speculated that Bobby Fischer died a virgin, or remained one well into his adult life. There was nothing on earth for him except chess. As a youth, fatherless and alone, he hunkered down by an old radio, whose music served only as a blanketing noise, a cocoon in which Fischer could curl around chess completely. That picture remained the same as he got older. After winning the World Championship, he departed the chess world, became a raving lunatic, and died in isolation and obscurity in Iceland.

"Yeah, Fischer. That guy didn't have a lot of fun."

What he was saying was true. Slow tournament chess, played well, is like violent meditation. The mind is wrenched by an evolving series of parenthetical thoughts, during which the limits of human cognition are directly assaulted. When it's beautiful, its beauty is deep and austere, and when you're playing badly, it's like slowly making out with a cold steel wall. Street chess, meanwhile, is hilarious. It's junk food. Even when you lose, it's funny.

"Now," Finegold said, "you can have fun with blitz games all you want. There are lots of those on the Internet. But you came down here to see me and become a serious student. You flew all the way down from Canada. You didn't come here to have fun, did you?"

"No," I said.

"Do you want to learn how to beat good players?"

"Yes," I said.

"Okay, good," Finegold said, "now let's play some chess, so I can yell at you."

We played for half an hour. While telling me how he was about to checkmate me, he texted his wife. Even though he told me what was coming, I couldn't stop it.

Marriage Is Okay

In the fitful emptiness that is downtown St. Louis, I was terribly in love with Katherine. Her immediacy in my mind was such that I constantly expected her appearance. When I saw a lengthening shadow, rounding a corner, my pulse momentarily multiplied. And when the shadow's owner appeared, I became angry, because it was never my girlfriend.

Before I had left town, we had been talking about getting married. As an abstract principle, marriage wasn't something I had wanted, because, well, there are lots of attractive people in the world, and I haven't seen them all naked yet. Also, though, losing Katherine was unimaginable, and she was going to marry someone, whether it was me or not. Much as I didn't want to get married, I also didn't want her to marry anyone else.

My level of confusion was such that it was affecting my chess. So I asked Finegold, during one of our lessons, whether he enjoyed being married. He and his wife, Karen, were extremely cute together. They balanced each other perfectly. She was a lovely, slow-talking Southern belle, whose genteel manner civilized any room she was in, whereas Finegold was apt to transform any situation into another absurd episode of The Finegold Show. Seeing them apart, it was difficult to picture them together, but when you witnessed their marriage happening in real time, it was weirdly logical. Sometimes Karen and I played blitz while Finegold heckled us. Their happiness captivated me when I was at the club, and when I looked at Facebook every night, I'd usually find a winning selfie they'd posted during the evening.

"It's okay, it's better than the alternative," he said.

"So you would recommend it?"

"Probably, yeah. I mean, I'm the kind of guy who needs a woman, and I think you are, too. Like, I don't know what I'd do without my wife. Kill people, probably."

"But what if it doesn't work out?"

"Then you get divorced."

"Is it worth it?"

"Well, my current wife is the least annoying of all of my wives. So, I don't know, I guess it worked out."

I decided that maybe I should marry Katherine, eventually.

You're Exactly as Good as You Are

There's one important, basic attribute of chess that I haven't mentioned yet. It's something I've always found exciting, but that also has frightening implications for the aspiring player. It's that chess is what they call a perfect information game. At every moment, you are informed of everything taking place, unlike in a game like, say, poker, where you're always at the mercy of an improbable card.

That notion might not immediately tantalize you. It might do the opposite, given that much of our entertainment is buoyed by cheap mystery. We're willing to watch hours of reality television to find out which of twenty-six people we don't care about is selected as a mate by another person we're equally unconcerned with. But before you dismiss the idea that perfect information can be an alluring quality, consider all the imperfect information games you play all the time. I don't mean only games like poker. I mean like the exhausting vagaries of interacting with anyone at all.

Let me give you an example. One day, in the rain, when I was in university, I offered a soaking person the shelter of my umbrella. As she said yes, I discovered that she was gorgeous. Her blue eyes met mine in pretty little moments as we went down the narrow street together, talking about very little but finding it somehow very funny. Being a more romantic person when I was nineteen, my imagination immediately overwhelmed me. Involuntarily, I was filled with theories about what kind of smile she'd smile on my pillow. All down the street, I heard in my head the words I knew she'd say after I suggested we might get married, playing out in parallel with our conversation. That afternoon's rain was a sunny one—her face shone in the orange early evening light. The air was sweetly musty, the kind of air I could happily breathe forever. Though it wasn't clear that my life needed saving, or what that would entail, I knew that she would do it.

So I gave her my number. She took it. She seemed enthu siastic about contacting me. Later that night, her boyfriend phoned me up. He was wondering whether I'd like to receive violence through a gun or a knife.

As cartoonish an anecdote as that is, I feel it's representative of a lot of human experience. Our lives are dominated by unknown elements—whether a stranger in the rain has a boyfriend, or who else has applied for your dream job, or how volatile the stock market is. And we try to make the best decisions we can, based on the information we know, but it often turns out that we know approximately fuck-all. Everything is dominated by randomness, and by accumulations of unseen factors. Like the dinosaurs, we rule our little kingdoms until a meteor shows up and unseats us.

Look beyond your daily routine and you'll find many frightening, unanswerable questions. Do you think your friends truly love you? What would happen if you took a right turn at the end of the road? If you had kids, would they be ugly? Would they treasure you, as you grew elderly, your skin taking on the texture of an old balloon? What will you die of? Is there anything capable of filling that tiny gap in life?

Much of the human world presents vast swathes of ignorance briefly penetrated by tiny, hopeful suspicions. Chess, on the other hand, is a perfect information game. To me, those three words sound like a prayer. The only mystery is how artfully you can process the clear, sober facts that are easily ascertained in one sweep of the eyes. While it's impossible to figure out how your life decomposed to its current state, it's very easy, in retrospect, to see how a chess game went wrong.

So, what are the frightening implications? Well, the perfect information of chess means you can't blame anything for your failure other than you. You had all the data required to make great moves. And then you did what you did, which is, in my case, usually not so great. That means you have to accept who you are, on the chessboard—you can't blame chance or circumstance.

But as Finegold told me in one of my first lessons, almost nobody engages in this self-acceptance.

"Everyone thinks they're better than they are. Everyone thinks they're underrated. Every game, they think they played badly because they were just in a bad mood, or their opponent got lucky and picked the right move. But it's not true. If your rating is 1200, that's probably where you belong. And you'll improve only when you stop making excuses. If your mood is really the problem, then it's not a good excuse—it just means you need to improve your mood. When you realize how bad a player you are, you can focus on the real problems in how you're playing. Being a winner starts when you realize what a loser you are."

What Chess Is Not

There was a child I hated, and I was playing him in one round of a weekly Wednesday tournament. I didn't hate him for any good reason. He seemed nice enough. But I felt a true and prismatic contempt, in which every one of his visible characteristics disgusted me. He was somehow the avatar of every struggle I'd ever faced in my life—both the trivial inconveniences and the sorrow like acid spilled under my skin.

He was playing boring chess. So was I, and the board was all locked up by opposing pawns smushed together. It was a pile of gluey slop. My rage intensified when he refused to be courteous and lose the game immediately even though he had a much lower rating than I did. This is not a good mindset with which to approach the game of chess. I gave up a pawn, and then transitioned into a losing endgame, which I lost.

At my next lesson, I explained my emotional turmoil to Finegold. He was having none of it.

"Your emotions are irrelevant," he said. "You can't stop

protecting your pawns because you're sad. Chess isn't one of those crazy stories that you sell to a magazine. You're not a hero; your opponent isn't the villain."

"It's hard for me not to think like that. It's kind of who I am," I said.

"Well, then don't be yourself."

Never Sacrifice

Nothing thrills the chess player like the opportunity to play a sacrifice. The prospect makes grown people giggle and drool like toddlers. It renews the weary heart and makes life seem worthwhile. A sacrifice, in case you've forgotten, is when you give away a piece, either for another, less powerful piece, or for no pieces at all. It's usually done to launch an attack—maybe you rip open the pawns in front of the enemy king by slicing one away with a bishop.

Sacrifices are so appealing because they're as close as you get, on the chessboard, to putting on a gasoline-soaked bear suit, climbing on a motorcycle, and jumping it through a ring of fire while ten thousand people are watching. Sacrifices are always a provocative stunt. After you sacrifice, either you achieve a brilliant victory or your bravery is proven silly. But beyond simply being provocative, the sacrifice exemplifies one of the loveliest truths of the chessboard: that it's a big world in there. Since there are so many possible chess games, there are many in which the most elementary principles of chess have been inverted, such that a humble pawn could be worth more than a usually superior queen, or even two or three queens.

You may have gotten a sense of chess's immensity by this point, but it's probably more immense than you think. It's a mathematically proven fact that there are more possible chess games than there are atoms in the observable universe. In fact, many more. If you add up every sequence of moves that could legally be played on a chessboard, you could assign a couple of billion chess games to every single atom. Admittedly, though, this number would then include lots of silly moves that no sane player would ever make. If you restricted the count to reasonable games of chess, according to the estimate of mathematician James Grimes, you would end up with a mere 10^{40} — enough that it would take the entire population of earth trillions of years to play them all, if we all paired off and played a game a day each. Of course, in a couple of those, a sacrifice makes sense.

Not all sacrifices are made equal. Some sacrifices, called "unsound sacrifices," merely create a superficial chaos that can be dispelled by prudent play. But sometimes unsound sacrifices work, too, if you can navigate your way out of the complexities they create better than your opponent can. This was the go-to tactic of former World Champion Mikhail Tal, also known as the "Magician from Riga," who just couldn't stop giving his pieces away. That was his whole style—he was always looking for an opportunity to sow chaos by removing one of his own pieces from the board.

He once said, "You must take your opponent into a deep, dark forest where 2+2=5, and the path leading out is only wide enough for one." Every chess player loves Tal for his daring, and tries, at some point, to imitate his venturesome style.

"Tal was good," Finegold said. "Tal could sacrifice. But you can't. You're not good enough."

"Probably not."

"Definitely not. When you sacrifice, you lose. Never sacrifice."

Never Play F3

Most of the time, it's not a good move.

Everybody Has a Plan Until They Get Punched in the Face

"What did I tell you last lesson?"

"Never play f3."

"And what did you do yesterday?"

"Um."

"You fucking played f3!"

I'd played f3 in a tournament the day before, against Aleksey Kazakevich, a far superior opponent, rated about 1900. It was one of my best games. The whole thing resembled a drawn sumo match—we fell all over each other, creating one violent, sloshy hug, canceling each other's aggression. The game ended in a draw. After the game, his son confronted him at the board.

"Why did you play for a draw, Dad?"

"I didn't play for a draw. He just made no mistakes."

Hearing this made me feel good about myself. But Finegold was not stunned by my game.

"Sure, you played good," he said, "but your position was better than his, and maybe you could've won. And then you fucking played f3!"

"Yeah."

"But, okay, you didn't lose your pieces. Good job. Very good. Let's talk about the next game, with Matt Barrett. I saw that game. I was disappointed, because you had a decent position, and then what did you do?"

"I played a sacrifice."

"You played a fucking sacrifice! What was my rule?"

"Never sacrifice."

"Then why did you do it?"

"I don't know."

"And you lost."

"Yes."

"This is my life. People pay me to tell them things, and then I tell them, and they don't listen. Even my wife. Every game she gets into time trouble. And I'm like, play faster! And she's like, okay. And then she sits there, staring at her pieces."

He sighed loudly and talked about his wife for a little while, and then started talking about me again.

"Look. I'm an idiot, too, okay? It's hard. Before the game,

you have this idea about how you're a great player. And then you get in there, and you're a sweaty mess, and you're nervous, and you forget everything you know. You know what Mike Tyson said?"

"Um, 'float like a butterfly, sting like a bee?' "

"No, he said everybody has a plan until they get punched in the face."

"So how do I deal with that?"

"You mean, like, how do you retain your plan when you get punched in the face?"

"Yeah."

"Get punched in the face more."

St. Louis Is Great if You're an Alcoholic

It was the day before my birthday and a few days before I left St. Louis. The thought of spending my birthday alone in my room, eating Domino's pizza, was awful. I wondered what else I could do.

"Is there anything good in this city at all?" I asked Finegold.

"There's more bars per square foot than in any other city in America, so it's good if you're an alcoholic," Finegold said.

"I'm not an alcoholic."

"Well, then you're out of luck."

On my birthday, I went to the petting zoo and hung out with some goats. I suppose I could've asked Finegold if he wanted to get a beer with me, but I felt unworthy of his company. Despite his lessons, I was still playing badly. Slightly better, but still badly. I knew better why I was losing, but I was still losing. He told me that this was normal.

"I can tell you everything I know," he said, "but absorbing it can take years. Chess is hard. Like, let's take a simple part of being a grandmaster. To be a grandmaster, you have to spend a lot of time thinking about what your opponents want to do, rather than just focusing on your own plans. Saying that to you is easy, but it's hard to do, because just thinking about yourself is kind of the human instinct. Being good at chess is pretty counterintuitive. A lot of the time, you're fighting your basic tendencies."

"That sounds hard."

"It's actually easy. It's just impossible."

Despite his reassurance, I still felt a little ashamed. Meanwhile, the goats were tranquil. They were accustomed to being touched. I gave one a hug, and it looked at me without obvious emotion and trotted away.

The Secret of Chess

After the petting zoo, I went to see the arch. On the east side of the city, there's this big arch, which is the most famous thing in town. The city calls it the Gateway Arch, which doesn't make any sense, because it's not a gateway—it doesn't permit or restrict passage. It simply frames warm air. One cool thing about it, though, is that you can go up inside it, and gaze out over a polluted river at East St. Louis, which is generally considered one of the worst parts of the United States.

"One, please," I said to the ticket attendant.

"It's closed today," she said.

"Why?"

"I don't know."

"Okay."

I was twenty-nine years old. I walked back towards the metro station, through the deserted streets beyond, between beautiful art deco skyscrapers, and I thought about what Finegold had said at the end of our first lesson. After we'd gone through a few of my games, he had nonchalantly asked me whether I'd like to know the secret of chess.

"Um, sure," I said.

"Okay, I'll tell you. But you're not going to believe me," he said. "And maybe you never will."

This was correct. I had no idea what to make of the secret of chess. And I definitely didn't believe it. Only later, much later, when I was walking on a beach in California, did his words really strike me with their full force.

8

I'D HATE TO BE GOD RIGHT NOW, BECAUSE HE SEES EVERYTHING

There are certain things I know to be true but that I can't fully believe. One of them is that failure is good for you—that it is, in fact, a necessary part of learning anything new—that, often, success comes out of a long series of mishaps that eventually leads to one moment of excellence. Believe me: I'm very acquainted with how progress rarely feels like climbing a mountain, and more often feels like getting stuck in a series of differently shaped sinkholes. But I still don't believe it, or at least don't welcome it. I want to be successful only, and I'd like that to happen immediately.

However, when I returned from St. Louis and started playing online chess again, it was clear that I hadn't taken a vast leap forward. I didn't become amazing at chess. I became a little better. My rate of improvement, thanks to Finegold's lessons, went from slight to modest. As the weeks fell away, I continued my slow grind, waged indoors, against online opponents, as a perfectly sweet Toronto July did its thing up and down the avenues.

It had been a year and a half since that first tournament game in Bangkok. The glacial sprawl of it all enraged me. And it enraged Katherine, too. We'd moved in together, to a pretty apartment that was just big enough that we could pretend it was big enough for two. In these close quarters, she discovered that dating a chess obsessive was one thing, but living with one was quite another. Often, long after we'd said goodnight, unable to sleep or contain myself, I'd creep out to the living room to play a few blitz games. Hours later, apoplectic, I'd return to bed as quietly as I could, which wasn't so quietly, so I often woke her up, and she'd then lie awake herself as I slept, wondering whether I was worth the price of admission.

I didn't want to languish in this life. I wished there was some way to speed things up a bit—some way to sell my soul to chess itself—some great and costly hero's errand I could embark on, with epiphany as its reward. But there was no obvious altar on which to offer myself. I didn't know how I could contact the goddess of chess.

There actually is a goddess of chess. Her name is Caïssa. She was first described by the poet Hieronymus Vida at the end of the poem "Scacchia Ludus," which depicts a game between Apollo and Mercury. After Mercury wins, he seduces a nymph named Scacchis and is so taken by her charms that he names the game after her. Later, she's renamed Caïssa in a different poem, by Sir William Jones, in which Mars invents the game of chess as a way to get her to hang out with him, which seems a little inefficient. From that point on, Caïssa came to represent the divine intelligence at the center of chess, who permits the game to continue only through her grace.

Many players have felt Caïssa's influence. Garry Kasparov would say things like "Caïssa was kind to me that day" after playing a masterful game. This was believable in Kasparov's mouth, because he played like a zealot, like a man hypnotized by a higher force, compelled to superhuman heights of precision and aggression by invisible cords binding his being. He used every bit of energy he had, and at the board, he exuded a barely contained combination of rage and desire, as if he were an intemperate bull forced to sit and have brunch.

I've never played like Kasparov, obviously. But I know what it's like when Caïssa is with me—when I'm studying well, when I'm playing well, when the game doesn't seem like a byzantine chore. It's a state of joyful clarity, where the possibilities of the board hang together like teeth in a smile. When Caïssa is on your side, she takes you by the hand and leads you through the many twisting back roads of her kingdom, whispering secret knowledge in your ear, and it all seems so obvious, like a memory you hadn't remembered that you'd forgotten. But that didn't happen to me very often. Her presence was inconstant. And somehow I felt, as the summer drawled away, that I had to summon her to my side—perhaps with prayer, or fasting, or pilgrimage. Yeah, pilgrimage. Pilgrimage is a cool idea.

"Fuck it," I thought, one day, "I'm going to go play a tournament in India."

India, I figured, was where I would find Caïssa, if anywhere, given that India was where chess was born, probably in the seventh century or so. It evolved there from a popular and disreputable dice game, Ashtāpada, the domain of desperate drunks and gamblers, a game that the Buddha condemned specifically for its addictive properties. Somehow, either a lone genius or a group of intelligent gamers realized that the game's board was the ideal setting for an imaginary conflict. The game they invented was quite similar to modern chess, but less exciting—the pieces didn't move as far across the board in a single move, which made the overall game much slower. Still, though, it was exciting enough that it outlived Ashtāpada. It engulfed the entirety of Europe and the Middle East in a few hundred years, eventually mutating into the modern game as players all over figured out how to make it more dynamic.

Historians are unclear about which province of India generated this devastating moment of invention. So I wasn't initially clear on which part of India I should go to. After some hemming and hawing over the near-term Indian tournament schedule, and entertaining all sorts of gimcrack ideas about why I should visit this place or that place,

I decided on Hyderabad. It was the most central of the cities in which a major tournament was taking place, and therefore, I assumed, the safest bet if I wanted to get somewhere close to the point at which all of chess began. (I did not examine the logic of the assumption closely.)

Also, conveniently, Katherine had always wanted to go to India. So we decided that I'd fly out to Hyderabad alone, win every one of my games, and meet up with her in New Delhi afterwards and do some heavy-duty classic romance, in compensation for the frustrations of living with me. I'd return ready for the tournament in Los Angeles, where I'd finally take down some 2000-rated nitwit and thereafter meet every moment of conscious existence with equanimity and grace.

■ ■ ■

I arrived after twenty-four hours of air travel, during which I solved puzzles as the clouds meandered below me. I stumbled out of the airport and found myself in an outrageous humidity that made me feel as if I were submerged in the intestines of an invisible whale. I paid far too much money for a taxi. It was immediately clear that I had done so when my driver burst into overjoyed laughter when I accepted the price he quoted me.

It seems to me that the way Indian traffic works, based on my experiences in Hyderabad and a couple of other major cities, is that everyone almost dies, all the time. Everyone with a vehicle flirts with their mortality extensively. All the cars slide around the road in patterns that barely accord with prediction, gobbling up vanishing slices of partly existing space. Between them, puttering motorcycles slalom and scissor in and out, piled with up to four passengers, none wearing helmets, all looking unconcerned. Everyone honks constantly, seemingly merely to say, "I exist."

Hyderabad is the center of India's emerging tech industry, which is to say that it's in a state of constant explosion. It roars with a sense of harsh aliveness. Crumbling old arcades are abutted by hastily constructed offices, swarmed by phone kiosks and fruit stands. The skeleton of a half-constructed metro line stretches above perilously tiny sidewalks lined with trash, and roads that are always overflowing. People are everywhere. It's maybe not the most superficially pleasant place, but the extremity is appreciably extreme. I was having trouble fitting all of the new reality into my reality holes. Time felt slow and squishy, and my few legible thoughts crawled slowly out from under the weight of a jewel-toned blur of sensation.

My hotel was organized around a square full of rebar and muck, encircled by mosquito-filled cells equipped with rock-hard beds and air-conditioning units that wheezed without effect. I was shown to my particular box, and I sat down and beheld the smeary walls. A few mosquitos expressed their curiosity about my body, so I slaughtered them without mercy. I looked at myself in the mirror for a long time, in a state of vague wakefulness, until I got hungry, whereupon I slipped away for a quick dinner at a dosa stand down the street. The owner, having established that I was from Canada, wondered aloud why I bothered to come to Hyderabad, since he spent his life wanting to do the opposite. He asked me if I could bring him back in my suitcase. I said I'd consider it.

Back at the hotel room, I applied mosquito repellant cream to my whole body, fell asleep, and woke up covered in mosquito bites. I'm allergic to mosquitos, so when I get bit, my skin produces a mass of tumorous size. I had woken lumpy. Before the first round, there was time for breakfast at the hotel restaurant, a small, dim, greasy room above the lobby where I scratched my tumors as two employees stood nearby, attending to my needs and staring at me. The breakfast of starchy puffs with sauce was delicious, enough so that I overlooked the fact that it was lukewarm, and thus probably not freshly made, and thus teeming with micro-organisms.

This would prove a terrible mistake. Naively, I wasn't overly concerned about diseases, because I'd purchased every vaccine available. I got the Japanese encephalitis vaccine, because, while chess is always hard, it's even harder when you catch an infection that makes your brain swell up and disintegrate. I also opted for the typhoid vaccine, because I didn't want to cough up clouds of blood during a highly technical rook endgame, and the *E. coli* vaccine, because vomiting on the board is generally considered distasteful. But I hadn't fully understood the degree to which Indian cities are hazardous to those who have grown up in a less lively microbial environment. It turns out that if you're not vigilant, you can easily pick up three contagions from a single meal.

Out on the street, I hailed a taxi, and as soon as we got off the major streets, Hyderabad instantly became beautiful. The murderous, spidering traffic spilled out on leafy lanes where cows grazed beside shacks painted in riotously alternating colors. But the ride jolted my stomach, which was already skeptical about what I had done. As I insistently handled myself all over, my cab rolled into the parking lot of St. Joseph's Public School, a lovely, gigantic concrete palace made ornate by railings painted baby blue.

Exiting the car, I looked at the time, and my fragile temperament shattered as I realized I'd be late for my first game. But as I crossed the long stretch of dusty earth bordering the school grounds, it became apparent that the tournament mysteriously hadn't started yet. About two hundred people were chatting and lazing about at the edges of the expansive courtyard, looking out at the hot air from plastic tables under awnings. As I stood there, comprehending little, an older man wearing a floppy hat approached me.

"Are you Canadian?" he said.

"Um, yeah," I said.

"I can tell by the way you walk," he said.

"Um, how do I walk?"

"Canadian style."

"I guess I can't argue with that."

"I'm Gopal."

"Sasha."

He explained that he lived in Canada half the year, and then got me up to date on all of his family gossip in a languorous manner. He didn't seem at all concerned that the tournament had officially begun.

"When's the tournament starting?" I asked.

"Nine o'clock," he said.

"But it's 9:45."

"I know."

"I don't understand."

"This is Indian time."

"What does that mean?"

"There is no such thing as 'on time' here."

"So, like, everything starts late?"

"Or early, or not at all."

"What you're telling me is that time is irrelevant."

"That is essentially the case, yes."

The game didn't start for another hour, leaving me to wander around the grounds, thirsty and confused and alone, as Gopal tended to his nephews. Except I wasn't really alone, because I had already made a whole bunch of friends. I had underestimated the novelty value of being a white guy playing a chess tournament in a non-touristy part of India.

Everyone was astonished that I was there. They stared at me as I paced back and forth around the sprawling compound. All eyes clung to me at all times. A few of the bolder young boys got up from their perches and started following me around. That encouraged some more boys to follow, and I soon had a little prepubescent entourage going.

"What is your good name?" asked one.

"Sasha."

"Where are you from?"

"Canada."

"America?"

"Canada."

"America."

"If you say so."

I then had this exact conversation with every one of them, while the others listened. They were all equally entertained every time. They started calling me "Canada," and started saying, "Hi, Canada, where are you from?" I tried to lose them, but they followed relentlessly. And when they grew tired of rediscovering my first name and my country of origin—which took a while—they began pelting me with questions of such menacing banality that it felt like a Harold Pinter play. "Why are you putting on mosquito repellant?" they asked. "Why are you wearing clothing?" "Do you like playing chess?" Some of them followed me into the bathroom, although not into the stall I chose, so I hung out in the stall for a bit, until I decided that the smell was worse than the kids, by a small margin. When I passed their parents, they gave me a look that said they were both apologetic that I was dealing with their children, and happy that I was dealing with their children.

There was no peace anywhere. When I retreated to the skittles room—the area of the building where chessboards are set up for casual play and analysis—my presence electrified the assembled kibitzers, who came up to me one after the other and pleasantly asked me what my name was, and whether I was from America. Then, after I conducted that conversation with each of them in turn, they stood there, smiling at me, as I studied.

After the passage of this eternal hour, the first game's beginning was announced by the shouting of a few of the tournament officials. The middle-of-the-road players, of which I was one, gathered in a draughty assembly room, at rickety tables set with old chess sets equipped with mismatched pieces. Our scoresheets, rather than being made from the yellow copy-paper I was used to, were held together by sheets of old-fashioned blue carbon, which immediately stained our fingers. My opponent and I shook hands, mutually smearing each other with pigment.

GAME 34 SASHA CHAPIN VS. VICTOR REMUNERATION

Victor was a kindly old man, who wanted to play some mean, merciless chess. But I denied him that opportunity.

One of the reasons that chess is a brutal game is that a single bad move can decide the whole affair instantly. If you're the World Champion, and you're playing a sorry jackass like me, and I play twenty random moves, I'll still win if you give up your queen on move twenty-one—there's no going back. Every move, over a game that can last six hours, is an affair requiring absolute concentration.

In this case, my opponent didn't realize that, through a simple maneuver, thanks to some clumsiness on his part, I could ruin the position he was striving for in the opening. Ten moves in, my queen was sitting right up in the crotch of his kingside—the area of the board in which the king usually finds shelter—preventing the vulnerable monarch from getting comfortable. I had him pinned to the floor and he was squirming around.

There was only one problem: the burping. In general, India is a place where, in comparison to Canada, there's a more nonchalant attitude towards the public execution of bodily functions. So, when one player in the corner of the hall let out a profound burp, it didn't occur to anyone that he had done anything wrong, and, in fact, a few other players, wanting to join in on the fun, started burping as well. That prompted a couple of older players to emit long spells of terrible hacking coughs. And since I was raised in a sterile, squeamish society where extremely normal things like burping are discouraged, this disgusted me and robbed me of all my focus.

In my confused state, I perpetrated a total fuck-up. It was the product of a weird cognitive phenomenon that all chess players know about—a particular type of mental blip that occasionally occurs during long tournament games. It happens when you're looking at a position, and you're sure you have the right move, and it's held tightly in the palm of your mind, having retained its promise after being subjected to numerous rounds of mental cross-examination. You're about to move your piece and hit the clock, but then you're suddenly interrupted—some unbidden cerebral current brings another move to your consideration, and you find it strangely alluring. And despite knowing that your original move was correct, you make this new, dubious move anyway. It's kind of like how, in an intimate moment with your loved ones, you think of something you absolutely shouldn't say, and then you say it. As Ovid once wrote, "I see the right way and approve it; alas, I follow the wrong."

So: all around me fell a plurality of guttural riffs. My queen was perfectly placed, dominating my opponent's army completely, preventing his king from finding safety. And then I did the obvious thing—I retreated my queen to a totally nonthreatening square, allowing my opponent to attain a completely comfortable position. Then, I lost slowly, over about fifty moves.

Outside, rain fell through hot sunshine. One kid came up to me and asked me how the game went. Then, another kid did the same thing. Over the next half hour, I had to tell a hundred people how I did, because everyone was curious about whether the strange, lonely Canadian in their midst could actually play chess.

"Why?" said one.

"I failed," I said.

"What happened?" said another.

"I'm stupid," I said.

"Why lose?" said another.

"I'm just not a good player," I said.

Over on the back porch of the building, curried lentils with rice were served on little disposable plates. Everyone looked at me. "Hello," I said to nobody in particular. A couple of people made inquisitive eye contact, to which I offered no meaningful response. The next game was scheduled for 1:30 p.m. It began at 3:30 p.m., after two hours in which I tolerated the weather and more socializing with juveniles.

GAME 35 COLD CUTS VS. SASHA CHAPIN

My opponent was rated about 1150. I was sure, therefore, that he'd offer his pieces to me, one after the other, and then give up. After the debacle that was my previous game, I was looking forward to a cakewalk.

There was only one problem: my stomach. Over the previous half hour, my slight thoracic discomfort had bloomed into a terrible bloat. I was carrying a toxic balloon in my midsection. My belly was full of indecent flora, having a party at the expense of my health. I wobbled around in my chair, pained and pale. My thoughts became fluttery and insubstantial, including my calculations—ridiculous moves that I would never otherwise consider became compelling.

In this confused state, I decided to play the Slav Defense. It was a weird choice, because the Slav is really complicated and requires a lot of study, and I'd never played it before in my life, not even in an online blitz game. Why I made this decision, I don't recall. Perhaps I wanted to be like Finegold, who's a Slav specialist. Perhaps I wanted to represent my Slavic heritage, even though I'm only barely Slavic, and don't care about representing my heritage.

Whatever the justification my harried mind stapled together, it was an awful decision, and my unskilled opponent punished me soundly. After ten moves I had made ten mistakes. On move twenty, he shrugged sadly as he delivered his rook to my back rank, and said, "Checkmate."

Back at the hotel, my ill health had transmogrified. My bowels had worked out their inner conflict, but now I was feverish and my sinuses were filled with muck. I breathed unenthusiastically until I drifted off. When I woke, I ordered milky, murky coffee from room service, skipped breakfast because the food was poison, and headed off to the tournament once again.

GAME 36 SASHA CHAPIN VS. RAJIV STILTON

Actually, my bowels had not worked out their inner conflict. In point of fact, as I made the first moves of the London System, a tedious but solid arrangement of the white pieces, I became increasingly nauseous. To be completely honest with you, my body was overtaken with spasms, and, as I attained a comfortable position on the board, I had to run to the bathroom to have an international incident, which took some time to elapse.

Outside the bathroom, there was no soap, only a rusty tap emitting spurts of dirty water. Also, there's not a lot of toilet paper in Hyderabad, and none at public schools— everything has to be done manually. What this meant for me personally, at that moment, is that I had to run across the road to a hospital and beg them for hand sanitizer, after doing some things I had to do.

An hour later, I applied some disinfectant to my be-smirched hands, and returned to find that there were ten minutes left on my clock. My opponent, who had a full hour and a half remaining, seemed happy about the situation. For the rest of the game, I didn't have enough time to calculate, or even think about playing well. And besides, my cogitation abilities had evaporated in the toilet. Being in this position, I just played not to lose. The result was a boring draw.

"How did you do?" asked Gopal, as we met each other at the chai stand.

"Badly," I said.

"Why?"

"Stomach trouble," I said.

"How did you do?" said a child, approaching us.

"Great," I said. "I played great."

This creepy feeling started coming over me—this sense that there was maybe an outside chance that this had all been a mistake. But I was too bothered by bodily sensations to be all that exploratory about the bigger picture.

GAME 37   LUCY STOCKTON VS. SASHA CHAPIN

This game was another disappointment. To give you a sense of just how disappointing it was, let's talk about Paul Morphy, the most melancholy figure in chess history.

Born in 1837, Morphy singlehandedly altered, everywhere, the conception of how the game could be played. He was a cherubic boy, born of wealth, with a gently sarcastic manner, whose talent was such that nobody had to teach him the rules, or tell him anything about the established notions of strategy. He simply watched his uncle and father play, and then beat them both, easily, in round after round, when he was seven years old. By the age of nine, he was one of the best players in his hometown of New Orleans, and conducted blindfolded simuls for fun. At twelve, he trounced professional player Johann Löwenthal, one of the strongest players of the day, in a three-game match.

Bobby Fischer called Morphy "perhaps the most accurate player who ever lived." This is a word that chess players use often, *accurate*. It implies that there's a truth to the game, and that a player's goal is to get as close to that truth as possible. Even as a mediocre player, I can attest that Morphy's play feels truthful—simple, unexpected, perfect. Kasparov called him "the first swallow"—as in, the first player who really flew.

What made his style different, if there was one thing, was a preternatural instinct about the relations between each piece. Whereas previous players, even the best players, had seemingly seen each piece as an individual weapon, Morphy regarded them all as voices in a complex harmony. With every move, his pieces became more tightly bound to each other, like a troupe of acrobats following a marvelous routine. And this symphonic understanding was animated by brute brainpower of the highest level: once all of the pieces were together, Morphy got them to collaborate with total suavity. He could calculate better than, evidently, anyone alive at that time—like Magnus, he didn't try to see the variations; he just did. So, he beat everybody. Adolf Anderssen, the best player before Morphy came along, was asked, after one match with "the first swallow," why he didn't play as well as he usually did. "Morphy will not let me," he said.

"Too beautiful for this world" is a silly phrase. Beautiful things are usually popular and successful. Unfortunately, it applied to Morphy's chess. He was too good. He had no serious competition on earth. Of the fifty-nine games he played against the very best players of his era, he lost eight. It's also speculated that he didn't take these games very seriously, based on the fact that he played very quickly and often appeared unamused. Many elite chess players refused to face him, out of fear. Bored of being able to achieve victory at will, he retired and began a law practice, which never became successful because people came to his offices only to try and engage him in a match. He always refused. His professional chess career lasted a total of two years. He died of a stroke at the age of forty-seven, lonely and idle. What brought on the stroke was a glass of water. It was hot and he got overheated after a long walk in the sunshine, and he drank a glass of cold water, and he fell over and died. "The ability to play chess is the sign of a gentleman," he once said. "The ability to play chess well is the sign of a wasted life."

If he truly believed that, he would've been dismayed to see how influential he eventually became. Even as geniuses after him continued to revise the character of the game, his victories remained the cornerstone of the chess canon. Every young player studies one brilliant casual game he played while watching an opera, against two dukes who insisted on harassing him as he tried to take in an aria or two. Morphy, versus their combined scheming, in the course of blitzing out moves distractedly, composed an attack of such inexorability and elegance that it feels like stars aligning. With every move, the dukes became more ensnared, putting up the kind of fight that a mouse does while being digested in a snake's stomach.

This is the ideal of chess that a lot of us possess when we begin playing. But often, when we start playing tournaments, we find that the chessboard is sometimes as full of dullness as it is filled with potential wonder. Unlike Morphy, we don't see the tiny opportunities that might be leveraged into a violent coalescence, so our games don't blossom the way his did. We sometimes just move our pieces around, shake hands with our opponent, go home, and despair that we're incapable of living up to the possible gorgeousness of the chessboard.

Speaking of which, there wasn't much left of me, four hours later, when the next game started, three hours behind schedule. Everything had been sucked out of my brain and intestines. I barely saw the girl of maybe twelve with a broad toothy smile who sat down across from me. Our game was unremarkable and protracted. The game ended in a draw, and by the time it was over, it was dark. A few more mosquitos had bitten my face, and I felt my muscles shifting under the new swellings positioned around my grimace. She yawned as she put away the pieces.

"I'm sorry I kept you up past your bedtime," I said.

"Do not worry, sir," she said, again with an ear-to-ear smile, "that is how long the game takes."

"I guess so."

"You are not well," she said, "do you need my help?"

"I'll be okay."

"I hope so. Rest well."

She got up and patted me gently on the head, and walked away. And as I sat there, after my forehead had made its way to the tabletop, I remembered something my friend Naomi once told me: "You put behavior into the world, you get behavior out." It's true. That's all you can do, and there are no guarantees of receiving any specific behavior in exchange for yours. Your love and fury don't mean you are owed a particular response from the indifferent cosmos. You can, in the name of chess, fly as far as possible from your home and get diseases along the way, and still be a mediocre player. You might take a pilgrimage and learn nothing.

Or you might learn something other than what you'd intended to. I might have come all the way to India to learn that I'm still the same mostly average person, even when titillating words like *India* are tacked onto my existence. That there's no other life for me that I can simply burst into by becoming excitable, at least as far as chess goes. That, like the vast majority of all players, I was probably going to remain part of the necessary lowest levels of the chess food chain. I was the canvas upon which more gifted painters could produce their violent work, like Paul Morphy's opponents. And maybe—maybe—I could improve slightly. But not by becoming ill in a distant country. There were no shortcuts, least of all this one.

Really, by coming to Hyderabad, I had broken another

one of Finegold's rules, right after I learned it: Chess is not some crazy story you read about in a magazine. It's the same everywhere, just like me. This was a normal tournament, and I was performing normally, which is to say, badly. All I could do was keep on playing.

GAME 38 SASHA CHAPIN VS. ???

I don't remember what happened in this game, which occurred the next day. I do remember that I lost. Afterwards, I sat down in the shade and the boys all thronged me at once. As they said words to me, I took a tube of mosquito repellant from my bag and applied some to my arm.

But it wasn't mosquito repellant. It was actually toothpaste. The boys laughed and started calling me "Colgate." In a childish huff, I stalked upstairs and sat down in a plastic chair, which shattered instantly. As I got up, one of the boys approached me.

"You fell down," he said. "I will tell your entire family."

GAME 39 RON DIESEL VS. SASHA CHAPIN

As I sat down to play, later in the afternoon, as the intense sunlight really began eroding me, I said, almost aloud, "Fuck you, I'm gonna win now" to the perfectly acceptable-seeming young man before me. And I played the Chigorin Defense, my favorite secret weapon, also a favorite of Finegold's. I don't know why we both like it. It's really bad, actually. But sometimes you just like bad things. Soggy fries. Hangover sex. The Chigorin. It's chaotic, risky, and clumsy. The only good part, I guess, is that your opponent can be confused by why you're playing so strangely. I ripped him apart, and he cried. And then I stalked off, thinking, "You're goddamn right." And I took an Uber back to the hotel and chilled out with the toilet for a couple of hours, waiting for vomit that never came.

GAME 40 SASHA CHAPIN VS. THE HOSPITAL

When I woke up the next day, one of my mosquito bites had a blister on it that looked exactly like cellulitis, which had nearly killed me in college. So this is how I would die—not in a sudden collision in traffic, but of mosquito-borne illness. I thought I was probably doomed, but I decided to skip the morning game and go to the hospital, just in case I could eke out a few more minutes of pained, perspiring existence.

I went down to the hotel concierge and asked him if there were any good hospitals around.

"There are very few good hospitals," he said.

"But is there, like, one good one?"

He shrugged. I googled the local facilities and went to the best-reviewed, which was just down the road, beyond a bunch of cows and traffic. It was a squat building, whose placards promised urological services I hoped I wouldn't need. I entered. The people at reception didn't speak English, so they offered me gestural directions that I was too stupefied to figure out. As I reconnoitered, looking for someone who could help, orderlies followed and took selfies with me.

Half an hour later, I was in a little examination room, being scrutinized by the first doctor I found who spoke English. Some of the orderlies who had followed me through the hospital—five in total—were smiling as they relaxed along the far wall, observing my ongoing demise, drinking thimblefuls of chai. The doctor concluded that I probably didn't need drugs, so she prescribed me four kinds of drugs. This was an approach to medicine that I appreciated. The pharmacist's assistant added me on Facebook after filling my prescription.

By the time I got back to the hotel room, my consciousness, such as it was, had mostly been scooped up by a swell of fever. It was much the same way after I woke up from a deep sleep. My unknown illness having reached its zenith, I skipped that day of the tournament and spent most of those waking hours lying on the cool floor of my room, thinking that I used to play frisbee when I was a kid, and now I was about to expire.

GAME 41 SASHA CHAPIN VS. NO-ONE

I did not expire. Also, the organizers had not received the voicemail I left them that declared I was missing a day and a half. Based on my non-appearance, they had forfeited all three of my games and withdrawn me from the tournament.

"But I'm here, and I'm going to play," I said to someone who was seemingly in charge.

"We do not know whether you will play," he said.

"Yes, but I'm going to play."

"How do we know?"

"I, well, I can stay here until the game begins, and then I'll start playing, which means I'm playing the game."

The man shrugged, and the conversation continued in that circuitous vein for another few minutes, until I gave up. I could've pursued the matter with the chief organizer, but, truthfully, I was thankful about being ejected, so I left. I did not say goodbye to the boys. Thus, Colgate disappeared. That was the end of my grand sacrifice to Caïssa, which had been grander than I had intended.

Back at the hotel, I thought I might spend the rest of the day analyzing my games with the help of my computer. Computer analysis is one of the defining features of the modern game, since, at this point in history, a strong chess engine is much stronger than any human player, and thus the highest authority on how you actually played. We've come a long way since 1997, when it took a giant mainframe computer, IBM's Deep Blue, to beat Garry Kasparov, then the best player in the world. Now, my phone could beat Magnus Carlsen. This development has also affected the way people watch professional chess: usually, during a high-stakes tournament, commentators have a chess engine running, which spits out analysis as the game goes on. The ramifications of this are weird: during a world championship match, the only people who don't know the best possible moves are the players themselves.

It's not always possible to absorb the lessons of a computer. All a computer can do is tell you what moves you should've played—it can't tell you, on a human level, how to think in a way that would lead you to make such moves. Nevertheless, I wanted to at least try to understand my dismal performance, so I could maybe derive some modest value from my week in Hyderabad.

But when I withdrew the scoresheets from my backpack, I discovered that this task was impossible. After they had rubbed against each other in the zippered back pocket for a few days, their blue carbon linings had shed, completely obscuring the recorded moves. My week in Hyderabad had become an indistinct blue haze, from which I could extract nothing.

I rubbed the scoresheets a little between my fingers, to see if the moves were still intact under the top layer of pigment, but they were not. All I got was ink on my hands. I went to the bathroom so I could wash it off.

At some point in there, I looked myself in the eyes. I was greenish, tired, and covered with a grimy residue of boom-town pollution commingled with sweat. My features, over-large and expressing displeasure, were like cheap decorations on sheet cake. How would the rest of this go? I wondered. Like, the rest of my life? Probably like this, because this was it. How cute. Running from one distraction to another. Finding any defined life unbefitting of a never-ending sense of grandiosity. Neglecting a good woman in favor of a form of comfortable self-imprisonment. Just like a few girlfriends prior, whom you'd abandoned so you could experience mental episodes in peace. This is how you are. You know all this stuff. And now you're spending all of your time learning it all over again. Super, super cute. Welcome to Hyderabad. It's hot here. The vegetation, though scattered, is pretty, and the people are nice, and they all want to get to know you, although the water pressure leaves something to be desired.

The sputtering stream of water was terribly cold. As it took the ink from my hands, it ran royal blue, and then aqua, and then it was finally clear again as the remnants of the tournament disappeared.

9

DREAMS DIE IN CALIFORNIA

What did you do with Katherine in India, after you met up in Delhi at dawn, at a cheap hotel whose entrance was partially blocked by a pack of sleeping dogs you crept gingerly around?

From a castle wall in a desert, we looked down on a city all painted blue. We emerged from slums where kids played cricket in tiny squares, and walked hand in hand along a river of sewage. Monsoon rain drove us down a mountain, through tea trees like giant vermilion sponges. The country's constant provision of novel irritations brought us closer, making up for my absence, at least in part. Also, I got sick some more.

Were you two okay, after that?

Relationships are always uncertain. But the prognosis was positive.

And why did you still play the Los Angeles Open a month later, after all that you experienced in Hyderabad?

I'd said I would, a year prior. It was mostly a matter of inertia and pride, the great movers of human activity. And, of course, I craved the particular way a pawn's crowning bulb felt as I played d4 on turn one. Maybe enough to get me through one more tournament

Were you sure that you really would quit chess this time?

I mean, of course not, I'm not dead yet, and all of my closest convictions have turned out to be revisable, such that I'm constantly turning to the person I was two years ago and thinking, "What a dolt, what a polenta-brained bozo." But it seemed like a good time to stop playing chess. I had wasted enough of my life. I wanted to start frittering it away on something else.

Was it really a waste?

Not completely, I suppose. Without a little friction, life is just lunch. Admittedly, some of it was certainly fruitless. It would be foolish to think I'd ever again benefit from knowing how to pronounce the last name of Russian grandmaster Ian Nepomniachtchi. (Roughly, "Nuh-pom-nuh-she.")

After chess, what do you see yourself doing?

Something warm and humdrum, like marriage, and the production of mewling children, and the attainment of a job-like job, and the purchasing of Christmas ornaments, which will shine on through the years as I slowly become, with age, less differentiated from the mass of other human beings, as everyone does.

Why?

I guess I'm fundamentally lonely, and I want to do what other people do, and have them approve of my behavior, and touch me or smile at me at the appropriate times. Basically, I'm dimly aware of the fact that I'm going to die, and I'd like a little tenderness before that happens.

But isn't chess a noble human endeavor, as you've said?

Yes, I do believe it. But that's not the only way of looking at my chess habit. It's true that it's a profound game, but profound things can, in practice, serve shallow ends. In a sense, being an amateur chess player is a terribly shallow thing. It's a long spelunk in a netherworld where there is no ultimate consequence, no permanent loss. For every humiliating game you lose, there is always another, as if your pieces were born again, fully intact, emerging from a remarkably fertile womb. In a single game of chess, unlike in the course of some other human endeavors, you can't make decisions that last as long as you live. It's not like, for example, a hypothetical marriage with Katherine, in which permanent bliss would be available, if I behaved correctly, if I didn't somehow recklessly extinguish our thriving two-person civilization. You can't start that kind of game over again, and you can't turn to a computer to find out what went wrong, or what went right. It's a learn-as-you-play kind of thing, despite the fact that you're playing for keeps. In this sense, chess was an escape.

When did you realize you should stop playing?
There was no one moment. Moments of realization are generally seductive lies concocted by unscrupulous memoirists. Typically, the process of epiphany is not instant—your mind doesn't just crack open. You usually realize something long after you've suspected that it might be true, after it's been lurking there for a long time, in the form of an uncomfortable thought that might have been droning in the background for weeks or years, like the purr of a detuned oboe. What we call "realization" is often the death of a self-serving rationale after it's been strangled by reality for a long time.

There was no one moment?
Well, I did feel pretty silly when I was on the toilet in Hyderabad. There's definitely something humbling about squatting over a hole in a distant nation, with your loved ones far away, and your lagoon-like thighs hanging before you, and the mosquitos hovering around you, waiting for the right moment to pump you full of malaria, while a young boy

outside is thwarting your plans, wondering why you were stupid enough to cross the globe just so he could trounce your inadequate handling of the London System.

So you don't think people should play chess?
No, I just don't think I, myself, should play chess. Empirically, chess has a ruinous effect on me. To others, I would cautiously recommend the game of chess. Just like I would cautiously recommend any temporarily pleasurable experience that might encase you completely, eclipsing all of your other concerns, leaving you useless to the general kludgy grinding of civilization, to the mealy pleasantness of everyday acquaintance.

Like drugs and stuff?
Yeah, like that.

Why did you see Los Angeles as a fitting setting for your last few games?
Los Angeles is where dreams die. All day, the waiters realize that they'll never be actors, and the actors realize that they'll never be famous, and the famous slowly dry out, under the nearly narcotic sun that falls on all the facades of the hot, sprawling city, clustered together in bright clumps like dirty candy.

What did you smell like in California, as you approached the hotel where the tournament was taking place?
Like pipe tobacco, amorous livestock, and a damp old forest.

Why?
I was wearing a perfume custom-made by Courtney, who skillfully interpreted my incredibly vague direction that she should make me a "chess-related" scent.

Courtney started a perfume company?
Yeah, a very successful one. And a lot of other things happened, too, while I was chasing my stupid hobby.

Like what?
The year was coming to a close too soon, as it always did, leaving everyone struggling with the question of how to interpret the fact that they hadn't done everything they could have. My mother went to some new fitness classes. My father got his flute repaired, and continued to almost never play it. My brother got a great new job. In other rooms, farther away, munitions were developed, embryos were tinkered with, and, lower down, magma tangoed around under the earth. Slowly, the universe was expanding, closer than ever to becoming a muddied gray soup of indistinct atoms, which would remain there for however long forever is. People I knew were more or less getting along.

And why were you wearing custom perfume?
So I might distract my opponents, setting them at ease with a sweet smell, lulling them into a happy complacency, a state something like the intoxication you experience at the crest of your evening's second champagne cocktail—a warm slushiness accompanied by a slightness of thought.

Did it work?
I'll never know, although I'd like to think so, because I paid a handsome sum for my perfume, enough that I don't feel like disclosing it to you. But it's so hard to tell, from the inside of a life, whether we can control our fate, or whether consciousness is merely the ability to observe ourselves obeying our irrevocable course, as if we were all self-aware pinballs. But I did smell pretty good, I think.

Did the famously sunny weather put you in a good mood?
Actually, on the first day of the tournament, the day was uncharacteristically cool and dim. Pelleted clouds thronged the sky, like Styrofoam peanuts seen from a compound eye. And though I tried not to interpret that as some sort of signal from the universe, I couldn't stop myself, because I was possessed of what I would call a toxically expansive mood, in which my mind constantly drifted rearward into an extravagant engagement with every available sensory stimulus. When I arrived in the hotel lobby, the ugly carpet outside the playing hall seemed to vibrate, to cry out to me.

Its celery-colored whorls seemed like a call for help. How I was supposed to help the carpet, I don't know. And, as I cast my tremulous face around the room, all of the players, however paunchy or haggard, blazed forth brightly, as if they were characters from myth, whose passing moods permanently altered history.

Why did you feel this way, even though you wanted to quit chess?
Animals can miss their cages. Chess had given my life a shape, and now I would be shapeless, at least temporarily, until I found another identity to stamp onto my experience, another temporary lodestar to guide my consciousness through all those bleak moments of blankness, such as when you arrive in front of a vending machine and suddenly discern a strange pit within yourself while deciding between sugared or sugarless soda.

Did you think you would find a similar passion again?
Frankly, I was doubtful. I wasn't sure that anything would totalize me as much as chess did. My assumption was that I'd live a life, thereafter, containing less totalizing passion. I was planning on having leaner, more manageable emotions, and occasionally craving the intensity I'd left behind. This happens to former addicts of all kinds, and they survive, so I probably could, too, I guess. In a way, it happens to everyone, with age—the volume of experience gets turned down.

How did the tournament organizers react when you announced your intention to play against 2000-rated players, after you strolled down the broad hallway off the lobby, past children playing blitz on the carpet, and all the rumpled older men reviewing opening theory on their laptops?

With a long spell of laughter, followed by a verification of my seriousness, followed by furrowed brows and an expression of concern. They thought I was making a fool of myself, and wanted to protect me. While it's common practice for aspiring young players to play up a bracket, in order to challenge higher-rated players, I was playing up *two* brackets, a sure recipe for a swift punishment.

Did you feel like you were making a fool of yourself?
No more so than usual. Chess is hard. Sometimes you lose. I would see what I could do.

How did you prepare for the first game?
By listening, in an unpopulated room off the main hallway, to Psy's masterpiece, "Gangnam Style," whose video contained dancers doing a fun horsey dance, which I performed gently there, on my own.

Shouldn't you have been studying chess?
In a way, I was.

How?

By resigning myself to the fact that I was as good as I would ever be. The only thing that could help me now was a mood of happy equanimity. Also, by dancing, I was getting some mild exercise, a preparatory step recommended by a lot of great players.

Were you worried about anyone seeing you dancing?

Actually, I was hoping that someone would. If word got around, among my competitors, that I was merrily hopping in circles, it might play into the psychological strategy that I had specially designed for the circumstances of the tournament.

What were the circumstances, and what was the strategy?

Given that my opponents were much higher-rated than I was, drawing a game with me would hurt their ranking quite a bit. And in a way, that made a game with me a fearful task. Every move that didn't result in an immediate win would make them a little anxious. So they had to play with a thoroughgoing vigor, mustering absolutely all of their brainpower. And they would hope that I'd play like most lower-rated players do when faced with a stronger opponent—that I would wriggle and shriek, with obvious fear, before their superior skill, and, in my delirious state, make bizarre moves, hoping that they would miss an obvious trick. But that wasn't what I was going to do. Rather than trembling before them, I would simply attempt not to lose all of my pieces, as Finegold said, which would forbid them from scoring an easy victory. And, while they stared at the board, vengeful and consumed, I would stroll around the room, or twiddle my thumbs, or just sit there and smile at them. In this, the moment of my greatest challenge, I would attempt to approach the board with seeming indifference, and play as boring as possible, with no clear plans other than blunting my opponents' plans, attempting the transformation of their eagerness into a confused rage. I wanted to make them feel like they were having a verbal debate about an extremely important issue with a banana muffin.

While you waited for your opponent, who showed up fifteen minutes late, what did you observe, as you looked around the room? I saw the lower-rated players quaking, and the higher-rated players doing nothing. Finegold once told me that when you're at a tournament you can actually tell who the high-rated players are just by looking around. And it's true: it simply requires a modest facility with body language. Strong players are the ones who look relatively untroubled. While they do feel a hint of fear, much like well-weathered soldiers, they're familiar with fear, and, out of necessity, have developed a negotiatory relationship with it. At this particular tournament, I observed Tatev Abrahamyan, one of the top-ranked players of the tournament, studying her cuticles. Meanwhile, the weaker players were barely concealing cardiac overdrive, white-knuckling their chairs, and generally looking like good candidates for psychiatric intervention.

Who was your first opponent?
Ronaldo Sevilla, a stocky middle-aged man with big, soft hands, whose combination of a gentle, untroubled face and an incoherent fashion sense gave him the air of someone who had enough familial affection in his life that he was long past caring about the opinion of strangers. He was, by all appearances, that most beautiful species of human: the quirky dad. He was rated about 1960, which, I decided, was close enough to 2000 that a victory over him, if it appeared, would comprise a fairly satisfying finale to my chess career, although not quite the numerical triumph that I'd been hoping for.

What happened at the beginning of the game?
I had the white pieces, and I played d4, as I usually do. He responded with the Gruenfeld Defense, which I didn't particularly like playing against. But I didn't really care. My pain and anxiety dissolved instantly as soon as he hit the clock, and it was replaced by a warm, fluid tranquility.

Tranquility?
The tranquility you get during a last fuck, or a last lap, or on the last day of a job, where the end is approaching, and you can only watch it coming, with your proverbial hands in

your sweat-stained pockets. Somehow, it's only when I am contained, in such a fashion, that I really feel free—when there is no point in resistance, when there are no alternatives, and my mind can simply resign itself to romping in the narrow province provided to it by a rapidly shrinking present moment.

What's the Gruenfeld?
It's a really tricky defense that a lot of people play, partially because Bobby Fischer won with it in the Game of the Century.

The Game of the Century?
Certain famously lovely chess games are given titles by the community, titles that are usually stately and pretentious, like the "Evergreen Game," or the "Immortal Game."

But why did the Game of the Century earn that title?
The thirteen-year-old Bobby Fischer, still relatively unknown, a little nerd with a radiantly wolfish smile, in a game against a much older and more experienced player, delivered an extremely picturesque checkmate after a stunning queen sacrifice—his first of many masterpieces. It was the shining moment that began his meteoric rise and tragic fall, and its biographical significance and tactical intricacy both give me chills, even though I've played over the game many times since I first saw it when I was seventeen.

Does chess make people go crazy in general?
Not usually. Most top chess players are pretty innocuous people. But it's possible that chess exaggerates negative mental tendencies in an unlucky few. It certainly hasn't had an entirely positive effect on my own sanity. Moreover, one could reflect on what was said once by early master Siegbert Tarrasch: "Mistrust is the most necessary characteristic of the chess player."

Did Bobby Fischer have a strong sense of mistrust?
So much so that he would order orange juice on airplanes and demand it be squeezed in front of him, so he could be sure the Soviets weren't poisoning him.

But couldn't the Soviets have put poison in the orange with a syringe, before squeezing it?
Probably, but even Bobby Fischer had to just relax and have some orange juice sometimes.

Why did you show the Game of the Century to Katherine on your second date, after you had enjoyed a few glasses of sparkling wine together and made it up to your small, grimy apartment, after wending your way through quiet streets awash in the aqueous breeze of early May?
Because, like all new lovers, we spent all our time talking hurriedly about our passions, so that we could feel the contents of our imaginations being reborn in each other's eyes.

How did she react?

Graciously, she nodded along as I raved for a solid hour about the intricacies of the game, and I thought that maybe this was about all I needed in life—an intelligent, compassionate woman in a sea-green gown who was somehow willing to put up with my bullshit, and a little cool air coming through a half-open window. I'd like to settle down in a moderate climate.

What did the game teach you?

That, unlike Bobby Fischer's opponent, I should respond to the Gruenfeld cautiously.

Cautiously?

When you play the Gruenfeld, you invite the player with the white pieces to occupy the whole center of the board, and then stab at them from odd angles when they're exposed out there. But as the white player, you don't have to take this invitation. You can set up your pieces more modestly, as if saying to the player with the black pieces, "I'm not interested in the vivacious, electrifying battle you want to have. Let's just sit around and do whatever." So that's what I did against Ronaldo.

How did Ronaldo respond to this?

With puzzlement—his large, ursine head lolled between his palms, and he licked his gums continuously, as if he were receiving transmissions from an electric device lodged in one of his molars. As we slowly maneuvered our pieces, without incident, he sank lower, until he was almost kissing his queen. He was clearly unhappy.

Why?
I wasn't losing all of my pieces, and I wasn't giving him any obvious path on which to proceed. There was no inherent antagonism between our forces, no clear way to gin up an attack.

Did anything ever happen, or did the game simply grind on forever?
After some shuffling, an intriguing position blossomed. We had collaborated in creating a delicate tension that might suddenly explode. Our troops stared at each other across a wide-open battlefield. His bishops, menacing and eager, eyed my hidey-holes, preventing the effective deployment of my rooks, but meanwhile, a bishop of my own threw its ominous searchlight across one of the pawns protecting his king, producing an annoying pin.

What did he do to deal with this pin?
He stepped his king out of the way of my bishop after thinking for a long, long time, and calculating all sorts of variations. This was his big mistake—it was this excessive cogitation that cost him dearly.

Isn't thinking good, in chess?

Not necessarily. Magnus Carlsen once said that he tends to play his worst moves after a long period of thought. Also, there's a classic saying among student chess players: "Long variation, wrong variation." Which is to say that once you've developed an involuted clutter of moves in your mind, you may have come up with some novel ideas, but you've also increased the chance of making a miscalculation, by dint of the sheer number of calculations you've made. So, rather than play a move with complex consequences that have to be precisely traced, it's often better to play a good, simple, clean move.

There are classic sayings in chess?

Many. Like, "When you see a good move, look for a better one," said by early chess master Emanuel Lasker. Or the witticism of another player of that era, Savielly Tartakower: "The winner of the game is the player who makes the next-to-last mistake."

Which classic chess saying described what happened next?

LPDO—"Loose pieces drop off." A "loose" piece is one that's sitting around the board without the protection of another. It's risky to have a lot of loose pieces sitting around, because they often fall victim to tactical blows. Especially, as it turns out, in a game against a lower-rated player with an odd smell, in a hotel in the far reaches of the San Fernando Valley, a few miles from desert mountains covered with flowering bushes.

Oh yeah?

Yes. Ronaldo, when he moved his king, exposed himself to a simple double attack—my queen could shuffle to the side and attack both his king and bishop at once. His bishop was mine. It was a rookie mistake. After I spotted the tactic and made the move, Ronaldo stared at the board in disbelief, stared at me in disbelief, and resigned in disgust. He then, in silence, showed me the moves he'd expected me to make, and walked swiftly from the hall, head low, torso flexed, as if he were nursing a sudden cardiac episode, which he may well have been.

How did it feel to beat a higher-rated player as a result of a stupid blunder?

I would've liked to have won with a feat of ingenuity, remembered eternally by chess scholars, celebrated by widows, children, and captains of industry alike, resulting in a fame so ubiquitous that household brands like Cuisinart and Hitachi would approach me for endorsement deals. But this was still pretty good. Also, it struck me as dramatically appropriate, after a fashion. My first chess tournament began with my losing to a superior opponent because I made an idiotic blunder. Now, more than a year later, after all of my stupidity, my last chess tournament began with a similar sort of game, except that this time the victory was mine.

How did the little Boston terrier at the residence where you were staying during the tournament react to your victory, after you returned?
She wanted to play fetch. I thought that this was as suitable a celebration as any. Then, she listened as I told her about the game and scratched her short head. We really connected on an emotional level.

Did you sleep well that night, even though you were shot full of the bright, acidic feeling of adrenaline, shaped by a mixture of triumph and melancholy?
I did not.

Did you underestimate the amount of food that would arrive when you ordered a deluxe breakfast at a diner the next morning, on the way to the tournament hall?
I did, and the flapjacks loomed on my plate, gigantic and uneaten, as I walked away.

Who was your next game against?
Darwin Mazzarelli, the highest-rated player of the division, weighing in at 2040, whose brown shirt was rumpled, and whose curly hair was spraying outwards with vehemence.

He approached the table breezily, almost at a jog, ten minutes late, and smirking lightly at everything, as if the world around him were merely an accessory to some infinitely diverting private joke.

What did he think of you?
I couldn't tell. He was undisturbed by my presence. He seemed like a man entirely at peace with himself. I wanted to hold his hand and somehow absorb his gentle, warm aura. But this wasn't some sort of daffy New Age therapy session. I had to beat him at chess. "Nice to meet you," he said, and then made his first move.

What was the beginning of the game like?
Sometimes, if I fall asleep with a mind full of detritus, there's a certain dream I have. I'm walking in a beautiful desert, amid scattered acacias, in the moment just before twilight, when a soft, agreeable breeze is palpating every surface. Without hurry, I approach the empty horizon, and I am completely tranquil, my mind a shining surface. But just as I relax fully, I become dimly aware that I'm meeting someone here, in this landscape—someone who has been following me, for hours, days, for my entire life. And I realize that I don't like him very much. Actually, what I realize is that I'm afraid of him, because I should be. I've managed to outrun him for a long time, but that's all over now. He's found me, and he's getting closer. Now, he's just over the hill behind

me. He's very fast. He can cross long distances in a vanishingly small amount of time. In fact, he's just a few yards away. And I'm too terrified to see exactly what he looks like, when I unwisely turn around, but I understand that he's a tall, handsome tormentor, perhaps an instantiation of Satan himself, the great deluder, filled with a malicious confidence that is entirely earned. In that moment, as he reaches out to touch me, I begin to scream, but my mouth is dry, and my tongue is slow, as if made of cold molasses. Then I wake up.

But, like, what does that mean in chess terms?
After what seemed like a harmless series of opening moves, I drifted into a hateful position that I was scared of. Accidentally, I found myself playing the Tarrasch Defense, a risky system for the black pieces.

Why is the Tarrasch so bad?
It's really not. But it leads to a position full of double-edged danger. The player with the black pieces—i.e., me—ends up with an isolated center pawn, which is, in chess, the equivalent of being lightly armored: unencumbered, but also vulnerable. The lack of an obstructing pawn shield lets your pieces dance around merrily, but if you're not careful, that isolated pawn can be captured, leaving you with nothing. And against a more skilled opponent, I didn't think that was a good situation.

Did the game immediately end in disaster?

No. Because, yet again, I played small, neutral moves, simply trying to ward off threats, like a dancer on a log. Essentially, I tried to put the ball in Darwin's court, risking nothing, saying, "Okay, come get me, you gentle prince." And, like my previous opponent, Darwin reacted to this with brimming effort, looking for some sort of lightning bolt he could throw at me. But he couldn't find anything.

Even though he had a superior position, after he slowly outplayed you over the first twenty moves?

Yes. We were playing for an accumulation of small advantages. And he had a couple, but nothing so dramatic that he could wipe me out instantly. Nevertheless, he was trying to find ways to end the game immediately. There weren't any, so he was using up all of his time. By the time we reached a complex middle-game, he had ten minutes left on the clock, and I had a comfortable forty.

And what did he fail to notice, as his clock continued ticking, as he gripped his curly hair, his evenly congenial manner now replaced with a steely, jolly focus, a stiff smile spreading across his face?

That while he was taking my center pawn—the event that should have provoked the collapse of my whole position— I was spinning up my own tricks on the other side of the board. To Darwin's dismay, I was engaging in what Germans call *Gegenspiel:* the creation of a minor chaos that risks making a twist in the game's overall narrative.

Like what?

I managed to snip off one of the pawns on his flank, and in doing so, opened up a long, pleasant lane down which one of my own pawns could promenade. And it did, immediately. It skipped up towards the far end of the board, getting ready to queen, with all the pluck and hope of a happy puppy on a mission. If Darwin didn't stop it, he would lose to the lowest-rated player in the bracket, whom nobody had ever heard of, who smelled like the exquisite secretions of a long-extinct breed of rodent.

Did that happen?

No. He stopped it. But, at that point, stopping it required the coordination of the only two of his pieces that remained after we'd traded all the others—a queen and a bishop, lined up in a powerful battery. Meaning that he couldn't do anything. He just couldn't move at all. However, being a clever man, he had arranged his queen and bishop so that they were also threatening my king, meaning that my own bishop couldn't move unless I wanted to get checkmated instantly. I was paralyzed as much as he was. We were locked in a mutual chokehold, our threats held in a delicate counterpoise, where if either of us did anything other than shuffle our pieces around uselessly, we would lose instantly.

The game was a draw?

It was. He poked at the position with his pieces for a little bit to see if I would do something crazy, but I refused to. We were locked in place. I had held off the most powerful player in my division.

Were you happy about this?

Irrepressibly, intolerably. After I shook Darwin's hand, and we nodded with apparent mutual respect, I ran outside and started skipping around the parking lot. My intention was to shake the ground with such force that all of Los Angeles County would feel my immensity.

Even though you didn't win, and your goal of beating a 2000-ranked player was still unfulfilled?

If you'd told anybody watching my first tournament game, in Bangkok, that I'd be able to slowly grind out a draw against a 2050-rated player, in a game in which neither of us blundered, they would choke on their milk. Even if they didn't have milk in their mouths. They would go find milk to choke on, perhaps sesame soy milk, just to be able to express their disbelief adequately.

And how did your joyful reverie continue?

It didn't. Because I knew that if I brought my joy into the next game, I would lose immediately. Joy was relaxation, and relaxation was death, and death was to be avoided, if at all possible. Instead, I ate spicy huevos rancheros at the place across the street. Then I crossed back over the sunbaked six-lane road, and sat down alone in a corner of the lobby, attempting to feel normal.

What did Darwin say when you ran into him on the way to checking the pairings for the next round?
"You've achieved very respectable results so far. Especially for your rating."

"Thank you. Usually I don't play well, but I decided to play well."

"It's that simple, huh?"

"Maybe. I don't really know. I'm just trying to play boring chess."

"We presume we know a lot about ourselves, but I think we live in ignorance."

"In chess?"

"In life. Good luck in the next round."

He clasped my shoulder for a moment, fraternally, and then walked off towards the tournament hall. After looking at his back for a moment, I followed him through the narrow doors into the carpeted expanse and found my opponent.

Who was he?
Jack Cheng, a nervous-looking twelve-year-old.

Why were you unhappy to play a young opponent?
Because children tend to play crazy, complicated chess, which was the right approach to take with me, given that my intention was to try to keep the game as simple and uninspiring as possible. Jack, I imagined, was going to force me into the complications I wanted to avoid, into the kind of fun I'd rather not have. If he was like most children, Jack was going to go for hasty attacks that would be easily dealt with by a grandmaster, but which would befuddle me, given that I was very easily befuddled.

Why do children play in such a fashion?
The minds of children are scattered and cavalier. They see far and fast with their slick, new, untrammeled cortices. But they're also impatient, eager to achieve triumph or simply any outcome at all. They play with high emotion, always attacking, as opposed to engaging in the flintiness usually displayed by truly high-level players, whose maniacal urges are suppressed. Children can see a checkmating attack ten moves away, but they display little aptitude for the slow, pedantic trundle of a nettlesome endgame. This is why players usually reach their peak between twenty and thirty-five: they reach an optimal combination of youthful agility and maturity. (After that, a slow decline tends to occur.)

How did the game begin?
With a limp handshake—he was socially awkward in a young, cute way, and couldn't look me in the eyes. And then, he played the Gruenfeld. I watched, amused, as our first eight moves duplicated, exactly, my first-round game with Ronaldo.

Does that happen a lot?
All the time. All over the world, chess players are doing the same things, over and over again.

In spite of the fact that chess is an infinite game?
Yes. Chess is both infinite and somewhat predictable. If that confuses you, think about chess as a walk in an endless forest. At the beginning of the game, the players enter the forest together, through a grand gate, and walk down one of a few well-worn paths that have been created by the footfalls of many fellow travelers—sequences of sensible moves that have been played many times before. But as they walk farther through the trees, the paths split, and split again, each time becoming narrower, as their route becomes less popular and thus cleared by fewer footfalls. And beyond a certain distance, they lose their way, moving off the courses followed thousands of times by others. They find themselves alone in a splintering space of permutations.

And once you were alone, on your own path, what occurred?
Jack, as predicted, threw his pieces at mine with zeal, in a
way that rattled me, although I tried not to show it. I flexed
my lips slightly so that they wouldn't tremble. His knights
tap-danced all over me, falling deep into the weak spots in
my position, locking me down so tightly that I felt like mar-
row trapped in a bone.

Did this equestrian assault finish you off?
Not quite. I wriggled, and jiggled, and, by hook or by crook,
managed to untangle my pieces and tickle his knights, sending them back into the empty tract in the center of the board.

And did he try to make the position complicated, once again?
Yes. But I didn't let him. Like a recalcitrant porcupine, I
remained curled and comfortable behind my barbs. There
was no progress to be made—at least not by a young player
of moderate caliber with apple cheeks.

How did he respond to this?
He just threw his pieces around with no apparent goal. They
somersaulted back and forth, all movement but no action.
He was baiting me. I was baiting him. Nobody bit. Our
pieces came off the board, pair by pair, as if escorting each
other to some gala. Eventually, there was nothing going on.
Our kings sat across from each other on an empty board. It
was an easy draw.

Two draws in a row?
Yes, and I was completely happy with that. A draw is a fine outcome, especially against superior players. Plus, as Finegold mentioned, chess is a draw if played perfectly.

Your game was perfectly played?
No, it was a clumsy ratfuck by grandmaster standards. But it was as good as the two of us could possibly do.

And then you left the hotel, and took a cab back to your lodging, and lay down in bed, and looked up at the ceiling?
And then closed my eyes, and felt a tingle disperse outwards from my thorax, a sense of love without object, until I lost track of the size of my body, feeling my toes carve an astronomical vastness by its joints when I flexed my feet. And I thought, "That is the crux of the biscuit," and vibrated deliriously, until sleep covered it all over.

On Sunday, the final day of both the tournament and your chess career, did you keep proceeding flawlessly, without a loss, demonstrating that achieving chess mastery isn't so hard after all, and that it simply requires a slight modification in disposition, achievable by any simpleton who is so minded?
No.

Why not?
The fourth player, the vengeful child named Miles Cheong.

Vengeful?

His aspect was sinister. His brow was permanently bunched. His mouth had settled in a smirk. He stuck out his chin in an attempt to be intimidating, which worked. When he shook my hand, his was bladelike and rigid. And he played the Dutch Defense, the choice of uncompromising players, who aren't happy with drawing the game.

What does Ben Finegold say about the Dutch Defense?

"It's not as bad as its reputation! It's not as bad as its results! You should play the Dutch against me!" He meant this sarcastically. Many grandmasters have a dim view of the Dutch, because it involves moving the pawns in front of your king immediately. You take a stab at your opponent's central position right at the beginning, with little regard for your own long-term survival.

Did this make your game all the more humiliating?

Yes.

How did it go?

Painfully, right away. Miles didn't brook my attempts to be boring. He swept his pawns down the board immediately, bringing the game to a sharp precipice. His play was dubious, in that if I survived his attack, his king would be as naked as a raindrop. But he wanted to disrespect me, to spit in my face, to shove his tentacles right down my nostrils.

He wanted to both razzle and dazzle me. And I was, indeed, puzzled. I couldn't figure out how to repel his advance.

Did you try?

I regarded the board and tried to grasp all of the potential complications. But it was a messy situation, and teasing out the possibilities felt like eating spaghetti with a clothespin. My tired mind shrank from the task, and besieged me with a spume of miscellaneous information. Chess is mentally strange, sometimes, in the same way that meditation is: When you stop moving and try to focus, your mind is hosed by bullshit from the inside. You're filled with recipes for pavlova, and the name of the capital of Burkina Faso, and the apparition of a morning you can't quite remember. It all comes back—all of those tiny scraps and figments saved by your memory for no reason at all. This does not help your chess. My clock was running down. I made a move. It was bad.

How bad?

It didn't stop his forces from crashing down the board and murdering all of my pieces. He destroyed me. He showed me who the boss was. He raided my fridge. He roasted my turkey. I was checkmated in short order. My second-last game of chess ever—just like that.

How did it feel?

Kind of exhilarating, like when you're filled with adrenaline following a spanking. I was high on defeat. Mostly, I wanted a cigarette. Or maybe I could sit down and have a glass of cold water in an empty room, on another planet where I was the only inhabitant, and laugh and tell the walls my secrets. But I had one last game to play.

Did you feel anything in particular?

I was feeling too much to feel any of it. My heart was thumping like a suicidal toad hurling itself against my rib cage. Or maybe it wasn't. I don't quite remember. It's a little like recalling drunkenness from sobriety. I remember that I was there, and that I was facing down my last game of chess, ever. This was going to be goodbye, and I certainly wasn't ready. Of course, I wasn't legally bound to chess abstinence, at this point. Maybe I would go back to the board one day. I hoped not. But I also hoped so. Hope was beside the point, anyway. There was checkmating to do.

Who were you playing?

Oliver Chiang, a young boy of perhaps fourteen, with large, sensitive eyes and charmingly stubby fingers. I liked him right away. I don't know why exactly. I just felt a sense of mammalian familiarity. I would've felt safe with him if we were two gibbons meeting around the watering hole. As I shook his hand, he smiled faintly, exposing big square teeth like polished granite chiclets. He seemed sad and exhausted. Of course, it's possible that I was sad and exhausted, and thus read my own emotions in his face. This is what they call "typical mind fallacy," the tendency to believe that others have an interiority similar to yours—that, for example, Oliver Chiang felt as exhausted in his adolescence as I did in mine.

Did he seem anxious about the fact that his mother was looming, tall and expressionless, vaguely avian in elegant heels, a couple of feet away, fixing you both in an unceasing gaze?
He didn't seem entirely pleased about it—after the first two moves of the game, he looked back at her, perhaps reaching out for some kind of signal of perfunctory maternal encouragement, but she didn't respond, perhaps not wanting to coddle him. She strode in semi-circles the whole game, remaining attentive and cryptic.

What shape did the game take in its early stages?
We began by moving into the French Defense, my old friend, of which Wilhelm Steinitz once said, "I have never in my life played the French Defense, which is the dullest of all openings." I generally agree with him. It's a dull opening, involving the creation of a little hook of pawns that locks in your pieces for ages while you devise some maneuver. But it's the one I chose often throughout my life in chess. I was fond of its enigmatic nature—it can twist off in all kinds of

crazy directions, although it can also result in tame, stale positions. Regardless, it was far too late now to turn back and live a more exciting life. After a few moves, we arrived at the solid Tarrasch Variation, which is eminently playable for both sides.

Wait, why is everything named after Siegbert Turrasch?
Because he's old. Back when he was alive, there was a lot to discover, and he discovered a whole bunch of it and slapped his name on all of it, being a somewhat arrogant man. Chess was a less-discovered country; its weather wasn't quite as charted as it is now. Now, in the present day, because so many brilliant chess players have lived and died, there are fewer earth-shaking discoveries to be had on the board.

And what kind of position developed?
A delicate balance full of hidden hostility. Like a freshly frozen puddle, everything looked solid on the surface, but would crack and gush with the application of any force whatsoever. Neither player had a safe or sure way forward. The pawns in the center, which comprised the board's binding architecture, were very weak.

Why did Oliver start vigorously rubbing his eyes, in a way that was faintly alarming, as if he were going to gouge them out at any moment?

If I might engage in the typical mind fallacy for a moment once again, I'd imagine he was just fed up. He wasn't having the best tournament. He had lost a couple of games. He had maybe disappointed his mother, and would possibly face emotional recrimination. This game might have offered a chance to prove himself once again, but now, like most of my other opponents, he was faced with unexpected difficulty. He just wanted to be left alone, and looked close to tears. I pitied him, and I wanted to give him a big hug.

And did he despair more and more as you quietly expanded your position, ratcheting up the tension, taking tiny amounts of space away from his pieces?

Yes.

And when he offered you a draw, prematurely, when the position was more or less equal, did you take it?

It was tempting. Drawing Oliver would mean I'd finish the tournament with a 50 percent record: three draws, one win, one loss. That would be an uninspiring but acceptable finish for a 2000-rated player in the division, but for a 1390-rated player like me, it would be like I'd invented a technique for cutting cancer with a toothpick.

What stopped you?

I was going to see this thing out. Oliver had no way of knowing this, but he was a profoundly consequential figure, and I wouldn't be happy with anything except a decisive result—a win or a loss. Chess would either give me a kiss goodbye or spit in my face and tell me to get the fuck out of its sight.

How did that go?

I pressed on. After some more maneuvering, the position had gone completely cold. There was no action whatsoever. The board had all the narrative excitement of a phonebook. But I combed the squares for some bit of chaos, trying to induce a mistake, or to locate the seed of some crescendo. My bishops scissored about. His rooks perambulated. He was suffering inside. His face, already paper-white, was paling further. Something was giving way inside him.

What was the tone in his voice like when he offered you another draw?

Quavering and high-pitched. He wanted to be in the sun, far away, in a place that required nothing.

Did you take his draw?

No. It was more tempting the second time around. But the voice of Finegold joined my own interior monologue—he had told me once never to take an early draw. "What if I reject a draw offer and lose?" I said, at the time. "I've lost more games than you've ever played," he responded, dismissively.

What did you do when Oliver's play became a little sloppy, allowing your pieces to gain access to the depths of his territory?
I went on in there. It was pleasant. There was a lot of room for me. His pieces didn't have a lot of space to maneuver, but mine did, and they found all the best squares. After some material was traded, I was in a much superior endgame, with a menacing pawn bearing down on his back ranks, supported by a powerful bishop.

You were winning?
Not quite. But he was presented with a tricky task. It was sort of like an interrogation. He had to answer a number of very serious questions faultlessly. And all I had to do was sit back and talk, and slowly grind him down. Without an absolutely virtuosic performance by him, in the absence of any major screw-ups by me, it would be over.

When he sank further and further into his chair, casting desultory glances both at you and occasionally back at his mother, what was the thought that crossed your mind?
That he seemed to be growing younger and younger.

Did you press on, moving that menacing pawn of yours up the board, continuing the slow squeeze?

Yes, and tears lurked behind his eyes and threatened to fall. I almost couldn't bear it. I wanted to tell him it was going to be okay. That, unlike me, he had a lot more chess games to play, and his whole adolescence still to set aflame, and then his twenties, during which he might live to traipse around Bangkok, or Nepal, or just find a series of rooms to occupy with a series of people. This moment, in retrospect, would shrink. It was barely relevant. In his memory, I wouldn't even be a secondary character. I'd be a tertiary sub-memory, with a face he could only faintly remember, if at all: an indistinct fog that he might recall and reinterpret two or three times before he died.

So were you thankful when, after about sixty-five moves had been played, he made the mistake of moving his king into a funny position, enabling you to land a wonderful move that you saw instantly—a stunning blow that would end the game immediately?

I was elated. It was the kind of move you dream of playing: strange-looking at first, but in reality simple and beautiful. By sending my menacing pawn to its immediate death, I'd uncage my bishop, allowing it to slice through his position and eat everything up.

But didn't Finegold tell you never to sacrifice?

Yes. But in every variation, I was winning easily. I sat there and calculated and recalculated. Plus, wouldn't it be wonderful to go out with a brilliant sacrifice? With a little tactical marvel, demonstrating how far I'd advanced? Everything dovetailed towards a momentary perfection of my life. I wrote "e6!" on my scorecard and reached up to make the move.

Why the exclamation point?

Chess players annotate games with punctuation marks. A single question mark indicates an inaccuracy. A double question mark is a game-losing blunder. On the other hand, an exclamation mark is doled out to excellent moves, and occasionally a double exclamation is given to scintillating brilliancies. When you're narrating a game and you're saying the moves out loud, and you come across a move that's so punctuated, you say "exclam," pronounced like you're referring to a former bivalve. I always really liked this, and the concept of "exclam" contaminated my non-chess mental life—occasionally I would find myself annotating a nice sunset, or the pretty face of a stranger, or the sound of wind on a snowy evening, in such a fashion. Exclam. e6! That was how it would end.

And how did Oliver Chiang respond to your exclamatory move?
He considered e6! for a moment, looked up at me doubtfully, and, in seconds, played the simple refutation, which turned my extremely favorable position into a losing game immediately. It was a perfect riposte. He smiled, a little abashedly.

How did you respond to that?
With a smile of appreciation, and wounded laughter. I could've resigned right then, but I played out the rest of the game blandly, trying to put up something of a fight. But I didn't really have any fight left in me, and there wasn't a fight in the position. His king just strode around, taking all my pawns, while mine chased after it uselessly. Now, Oliver had grown out of the temporary infancy into which he had plunged, seeming like a commanding young man, full of gravitas and energy, and I felt very, very old.

And what did you and Oliver say, after he checkmated you, twenty elementary moves later?
"You could've won," he said, somewhat in disbelief.

"I know," I said.

"You were playing really well. If you made any other move I'd be dead."

"It's okay."

"Sorry."

"Thanks for the game."

We shook hands.

Was it actually okay?
Sure. In the same way that it was okay that all human affairs come to nothing, eventually. It was okay because it had to be. My chess career ended with an unsound sacrifice, refuted by a child. He walked away happy and tired. I was pleased to have pleased him.

■■■

In a few minutes, my Uber driver, Natasha, picked me up from the parking lot in front of the hotel. She was lovely, asking me, "Where you goin', baby?" even though her GPS clearly told her where I was going. I had rented a little room by the ocean. Not because I wanted, now that chess was over, to jump in the waves and never be seen again, although that image had occurred to me. I just felt like I deserved to see some pretty water—some celebrated, high-quality California water—while it was available. I had come this far. Why not go a little farther?

It was a long drive south, down towards Los Angeles proper and its horizon-touching multitude of lights. The spread of squared-away incandescence made me feel so small—it seemed to me like a graph of human possibility, each point representing a different end. My brief dalliance with the tournament chess scene was such a big deal when I was in it, but right then, as I saw the approach of so much electricity, I couldn't honestly claim that it was anything other than infinitesimal.

Natasha was chatty, but I didn't want to talk to anybody, so I responded in monosyllables to a few of her kind questions, until she realized that both of us would be better served by silence. I just wanted to feel the dumb feelings I was feeling: momentary hiccups of happiness, replaced quickly by dull pains, a combination that I understood to be nostalgia for the present—I was already longing for the current moment, as I felt it flaking away. However, despite my sullenness, I knew Finegold and Katherine probably wanted to hear from me, so I sent them some messages.

"Nice," Finegold wrote, in response. We talked about this and that—he had seen a Facebook post about my trip to India, and he shared some anecdotes about the intestinal troubles he had also suffered there. "I'm so proud of you," Katherine wrote, probably happy that all of this was over. I guess I was happy, too. I guess it was mostly fine. This was, most likely, as good at chess as I'd ever be—this was all the satisfaction I'd get. It wasn't clear whether it was enough. "Enough," as applied to something you love, is a poorly defined concept.

The bright moon didn't seem to mind very much that I began crying a little, quietly, in the back seat. I thought it would be surprised, like I was—I'm not much of a crier. "Have a good night, baby," Natasha said, as she parked and

I got out. It's so amazing, the way some American women can say "baby" in a harmless, nonsexual way, as if you are a literal baby that they're going to take care of. Maybe I could achieve a similar effect, if I practiced. There was a lot of time for hobbies, now—many hours that would be howling for some kind of substance. I walked down to the beach.

10

THE BEACH

My firm belief is that it's important to discover your own tremendous lack of potential. Life often contains the discovery that your place in humanity isn't quite what you thought it was. You find out that you weren't meant to be the lover of the thing you first loved. But it's not so bad. If you're lucky, you end up loving something else. When failure removes you from the wrong path, as wrenching as that feels, you ought to be grateful. You're a little closer to where you should be, even if you don't know where that is yet. Given the choice of any profession whatsoever, I would choose chess genius. I wasn't given that choice.

Now that we've established that, I guess I should reveal the secret of chess. But you should know that I'm a little nervous about telling it to you. It means so much to me, and it's always nerve-racking when you tell a friend a secret you find precious. You want it to illuminate their mind with ineffable light, but sometimes it doesn't, and they just look at you as if they're still waiting for the quintessential information you had promised.

But here we are, under a few exhausted stars, on the wide, flat beach, a half-mile south of the Venice pier. The sand is dark gray in the faint, nearly midnight light, and the water that embraces it is blue-black, and it's cold out, and I didn't think to pack a sweater. I should really get this over with, so I can go inside and text Katherine.

At the end of my first lesson with Finegold, he nonchalantly asked me whether I'd like to know the secret of chess.

"Um, sure," I said.

"Okay, I'll tell you. But you're not going to believe me," he said. "And maybe you never will."

I nodded.

"You have to play like you never want the game to end," he said.

And he was right. I didn't believe him. But I asked him to tell me more.

"In life, and in chess, people make terrible decisions just because they're impatient. They want things to end, right now, on their terms. They just want a reckoning, whether or not it's actually good. So they play f4, or they play bishop takes h7, and they just tear everything apart. But you don't have to play that way. You can play for hundreds of moves, if you want to. You could play for a thousand. And if you're happy with that, your opponent will be like, I want a sand-wich, I want a beer, I want to get out of here. But mean-while, you're content. You don't have to go anywhere. You just like moving the pieces around. You just like playing chess."

I don't recall what my face did in response, but it did something.

"Okay, see you next week," he said.

And as I bought some coconut water afterwards, his words swelled up inside me, monolithic and strange. Al-though I didn't know what to make of them, I knew they were significant somehow, and they stuck in my memory, and came back to me at odd hours of the day, all through-out that summer. Gradually, I realized that Finegold's words contained not only a philosophy of chess, but also an idea of heaven. How beautiful it would be, I realized, to be playing a game without ever wanting it to be over.

I had never felt that before. I certainly never achieved that peace on the chessboard. I never felt secure. I was always playing f4, or bishop takes h7, or trying to land a brilliant tac-tical blow against Oliver Chiang. Even in the most exquisite moments of my life, I had always wanted to leave for some-where else, or be something different. Even in the middle of ecstasy, there was always something else calling me: some algae-covered cove, or the Chigorin Defense. It might not be right to live this way. After all, everything I care for was born dying, and I can't be everything I want. In fact, I can barely be anything at all. I would have to stay somewhere at some point.

This could be all right, honestly, in this rented bedroom overlooking the ocean. A little dog is barking in the hallway, and it's just become Monday. Katherine could fly down here tomorrow, and we could live some kind of life together. Outside, people on the street are making confessions, which are half-erased by the wind by the time they reach me. The glow of all the city's neon falls on everything I'm not thinking about right now.

The only purpose here is amusement, I suppose, and the rules are completely unclear. Love is nice. You can kiss someone, and have a little cake right before oblivion. It's a dream that ends before you know what it all added up to. It's scary if you worry about it. But if you're lucky, maybe you'll like it, eventually. You just like moving the pieces around, thinking, this is okay. I enjoy this game. It's different, even if it's a lot like all the others. It's almost over, but I'm in no hurry. I could happily play a little while longer. Please don't make me go.

ACKNOWLEDGMENTS

I have been aided by a many-tendrilled human network that is too large for my small mind to grasp at any one time. So, if I've forgotten you in this list but owe you gratitude, please assume that the omission is a product of stupidity rather than any ill feeling.

My current life would have been categorically impossible without the personal support provided by my family (Avivah Wargon, Elliott Chapin, Sam Chapin), as well as Anna Gallagher-Ross, D'Arcy Henderson, Stephen Thomas, Naomi Skwarna, Jackie Grandy, Darrah Teitel, Courtney Rafuse, and Katherine Laidlaw.

In terms of professional stuff: Haley Cullingham single-handedly started my career and also contributed greatly to this book. Without her, none of this. Also instrumental: Jen Agg blessed me with her immense power. My genius agent Martha Webb was my constant advocate and guide and was necessary. Jenny Bradshaw was ruthlessly intelligent and was always the exact right mix of velvet glove and iron fist in the editorial process. Jared Bland pulled the strings beautifully, as he always does. Kristin Cochrane pointed an imperious finger and this book sprang into being. Andrew Roberts made it look so, so pretty. Tara Tovell executed the unglamorous and difficult task of legitimizing my comma use. And Yaniv Soha gave this strange thing another home.

Along the way, housing arrangements were provided by, in chronological order, Elena Gartner, Sally Mairs, Hermes Huang, Puja Singh, Praveen Kumar Yadav, Patrick Ward, Tenzin Seldon, Connor Moran, Michele Moses, Luca Piccin, Caroline Daren, Sofie Belkin-Sessler, Charity Chan, Fawn Parker, Oliver Cheng, Amirah El-Safty, Amelia Roblin, Emma van Ryn, Sebastian Riopel Murray, Jade Blair, Kate Browning, Dave Frank-Savoie, Matthew Sharp, Andrew Parks, Puja Singh, and especially Amy and Tom Klein. Thanks for letting me sleep in your places, guys.

Readers! Thanks for the savagery and compliments when both were needed. Uri Bram, Karen Dawson, Tedde Albertson, Aella, Ben Deeb.

Ben Finegold was incredibly cooperative, except on the chessboard, and for that I will be eternally indebted.

Alex Manley, Arun Kirupanathan, Danny Viola, and Nitsuh Abebe: thank you for the employment. It was good to be able to feed myself.

Victoria Lynn Hogan: you came in late in the process, but your contribution was incalculably vital.

Last, but maybe not least, thank you to Vassily Ivanchuk for all of your innovations in chess and fashion, and thank you to Imo's Pizza for being so committed to your bizarre culinary ideals.